U.S. Geological Survey

Maps and Descriptions of Routes of Exploration in Alaska in 1898

With General Information Concerning the Territory

U.S. Geological Survey

Maps and Descriptions of Routes of Exploration in Alaska in 1898
With General Information Concerning the Territory

ISBN/EAN: 9783337143527

Printed in Europe, USA, Canada, Australia, Japan

Cover: Foto ©Andreas Hilbeck / pixelio.de

More available books at **www.hansebooks.com**

55TH CONGRESS, } SENATE. { DOCUMENT
3d Session.   }   { No. 172.

DEPARTMENT OF THE INTERIOR
UNITED STATES GEOLOGICAL SURVEY
CHARLES D. WALCOTT, DIRECTOR

MAPS AND DESCRIPTIONS

OF ROUTES OF

EXPLORATION IN ALASKA

IN 1898

WITH GENERAL INFORMATION CONCERNING THE TERRITORY

(TEN MAPS IN ACCOMPANYING ENVELOPE)

PREPARED IN ACCORDANCE WITH PUBLIC RESOLUTION No. 25 OF THE FIFTY-FIFTH CONGRESS
THIRD SESSION, APPROVED MARCH 1, 1899

PRINTED IN THE ENGRAVING AND PRINTING DIVISION OF THE
UNITED STATES GEOLOGICAL SURVEY
WASHINGTON, D. C.
1899

CONTENTS.

	PAGE.
SUMMARY OF PLANS AND RESULTS, BY THE DIRECTOR	11

PART I.—SPECIAL REPORTS OF EXPEDITIONS.

Report of the Sushitna expedition, by G. H. Eldridge and Robert Muldrow	15
General topographic features of the route	15
Geology	19
Formations	19
Granite	19
Sushitna slate series	20
Cantwell conglomerate	20
Kenai series	20
Recent deposits	21
Eruptives	21
Structure	21
Mineral resources	22
Gold	22
Coal	22
Possibilities of agriculture	24
Climate	24
Temperature and weather observations in 1898	25
Weather conditions in 1897	25
Routes to the interior	26
Magnetic variations, Sushitna River, 1898	27
Report of the Kuskokwim expedition, by J. E. Spurr and W. S. Post	28
Itinerary	28
Topography	29
Cook Inlet	29
Skwentna region	30
Kuskokwim region	30
Kanektok region	31
Togiak region	31
Nushagak region	31
Naknek region	31
Population	31
Climate	32
Vegetation and birds	33
Game and fish	34
Geology	34
Résumé	36
Mineral resources	36
Land and water routes	37

3

	PAGE.
Table of distances along route from Tyonek to Katmai	38
Magnetic variations, southwestern Alaska, 1898	39
Report on the region between Resurrection Bay and the Tanana River, by W. C. Mendenhall	40
Introduction	40
Geography and topography	41
Cook Inlet and Prince William Sound	41
General topography	41
Routes	43
Methods of travel	44
General geology	45
Sunrise series	45
Age	45
Matanuska series	46
Age	46
Greenstone series	46
Tanana series	46
Known gold districts	47
Turnagain Arm	47
Matanuska Valley	47
General gravel sheet	47
Coal	48
Timber and grass	48
Game	49
Climate	49
Agriculture	50
Inhabitants	50
Report on Prince William Sound and the Copper River region, by F. C. Schrader	51
Itinerary	51
Geography	52
Population	52
Prince William Sound natives	52
Prince William Sound whites	52
Copper River natives	52
Prospectors and explorers	53
Climate	53
Prince William Sound	53
Valdez summit	54
Copper River district	54
Animal life	54
Fish	54
Quadrupeds	54
Birds	54
Insects	55
Vegetation	55
Prince William Sound	55
Copper River district	55
Topography	55
Geology	57
Orca series	57
Valdez series	57
Age of the Valdez and Orca series	57

CONTENTS.

	PAGE.
Copper Mountain greenstone or amphibolite-schist	57
Klutena series	58
Igneous rocks	58
Copper River silts	58
Mineral resources	59
Copper	59
Copper Mountain mine	59
Gladhaugh Bay mine	59
Latouche and Knights islands	59
Gold-bearing quartz	60
Placers	60
Coal	61
Routes and trails	61
Table of approximate distances by Glacier trail	63
Report of the White River-Tanana expedition, by W. J. Peters and Alfred H. Brooks	64
Narrative	64
Previous explorations	65
Geography	65
Geology	67
Nasina series	67
Basal gneissoid series	68
Tanana schists	68
Wellesley formation	68
Nilkoka formation	68
Younger sedimentary rocks	68
Igneous rocks	69
Summary of the bed rock geology	69
Glacial phenomena	69
Silts and gravels	69
Volcanic ash	69
Mineral resources	70
Gold	70
Copper	71
Coal	71
Timber	71
Game	71
Climate	72
Agriculture	72
Routes and means of transportation	72
White River	72
Trails to White River	73
Tanana River	73
Trails to the Tanana	73
Railway routes	74
Inhabitants	74
Whites	74
Indians	74
Marks and monuments along the route of travel	74
Table of approximate distances	75
Magnetic declinations	75
Report of the Fortymile expedition, by E. C. Barnard	76
Itinerary	76

	PAGE
Methods of work	78
Topography	78
Routes	79
Methods of travel	80
Population	80
Mining activity	80
Gold	80
Coal	81
Soda springs	81
Climate	81
Timber	82
Food resources	82

PART II.—GENERAL INFORMATION CONCERNING THE TERRITORY; BY GEOGRAPHICAL PROVINCES.

The Yukon district, by Alfred H. Brooks	85
Geography	85
Limits of the Yukon drainage basin	85
Yukon plateau	86
Rivers of the Yukon Basin	86
The main Yukon River	87
Koyukuk River	87
Tanana River	88
Porcupine River	88
White River	89
Pelly and Lewes rivers	89
Geology	89
Rock formations	89
Glaciation	91
Recent volcanic activity	91
Mineral resources	91
Gold	91
Gold Mountain	92
Mynook district	92
Birch Creek district	92
Seventymile district	93
Mission Creek district	93
Fortymile district	93
Sixtymile district	93
Koyukuk district	93
Porcupine River	94
Klondike district	94
Other gold districts of British Northwest Territory	95
Atlin Lake district	95
Dalton trail region	95
Coal	95
Timber	95
Game	96
Climate	96
Routes and means of transportation	96
Chilkoot and White Pass routes	97
St. Michael route	97

	PAGE.
Dalton trail	98
Taku, Stikine, Edmonton, and Copper River routes	98
Winter travel	98
Population	99
Table of approximate distances, Lewes and Yukon rivers	100
The extreme southeastern coast, by G. H. Eldridge	101
The coast from Lynn Canal to Prince William Sound, by G. H. Eldridge	103
Lituya Bay	103
Yakutat	103
Chilkat coal field	103
Kayak and Little Kayak islands	104
Middleton Island	104
The Prince William Sound and Copper River country, by F. C. Schrader	105
Topography	105
Routes	105
Explorations	106
Native population	107
Prospectors and adventurers	107
Resources	107
Climate and vegetation	108
The Kenai Peninsula, by W. C. Mendenhall	109
Topography	109
Inhabitants	109
Geology	110
Gold	110
Coal	110
The Sushitna drainage area, by G. H. Eldridge	111
Topography and general features	111
Geology	111
Mineral resources	111
Agriculture	112
Routes	112
The Kadiak Islands, by W. C. Mendenhall	113
General description	113
Geology and mineral resources	113
The Alaska Peninsula and the Aleutian Islands, by W. C. Mendenhall	115
Geography	115
Geology	115
Gold	116
Coal	116
Routes across the peninsula	117
Inhabitants and industries	117
Villages	117
Lakes Iliamna and Clark, by J. E. Spurr	118
The Nushagak River, by J. E. Spurr	119
The coast from Bristol Bay to the Yukon, by J. E. Spurr	120
Topography	120
Population	120
Settlements	120
Pribilof Islands	121
The Kuskokwim drainage area, by J. E. Spurr	122
Topography	122
Routes	122

	PAGE.
Explorations	122
Population	123
Resources	123
From the Yukon Mouth to Point Barrow, by J. E. Spurr	124
Topography	124
Explorations	124
Norton Sound	125
St Lawrence Island	125
Cape Prince of Wales and vicinity	125
Kotzebue Sound	125
Point Hope to Point Barrow	126
The Kowak River, by J. E. Spurr	127
The Noatak River, by J. E. Spurr	129
The coast from Point Barrow to the Mackenzie, by Alfred H. Brooks.	130

PART III.—TABULATED INFORMATION.

Meteorological tables	133
Mean temperature	133
Extremes of temperature, maximum	134
Extremes of temperature, minimum	134
Precipitation	135
Periods during which certain Alaskan rivers are free from ice	136
Report of Postal Service in operation in Alaska, March, 1899	136
Postal routes	136
Post-offices established	137
United States land offices	138
Gold production of Alaska, by districts	138
Ration list adopted by J. E. Spurr	138

LIST OF MAPS.

(*In separate envelope.*)

1. General chart of Alaska.
2. Sushitna River and adjacent territory.
3. Head waters of Skwentna and Kuskokwim rivers.
4. Middle Kuskokwim River, south to Bristol Bay and Togiak River.
5. Lower Kuskokwim River and Kanektok River.
6. Knik Arm to Tanana River via Matanuska and Delta rivers.[1]
7. Copper River and Klutena Lake.[1]
8. Prince William Sound.
9. Tanana and White rivers.
10. Fortymile quadrangle.

---

[1]Through the courtesy of Hon. G. D. Meiklejohn, Assistant Secretary of War, the maps prepared in connection with the expeditions to Alaska under Captains Glenn and Abercrombie are published herewith.

MAPS AND DESCRIPTIONS OF ALASKA.

SUMMARY OF PLANS AND RESULTS.

By THE DIRECTOR.

In January, 1898, Congress provided $20,000 for surveys in Alaska by the United States Geological Survey. In pursuance of this legislation several expeditions of geologists and topographers were organized. The parties were outfitted in Seattle, Washington, under the direction of Mr. G. H. Eldridge, geologist, and sailed northward on the United States gunboat *Wheeling* on April 5. The officers assigned to the expedition were Messrs. G. H. Eldridge, J. E. Spurr, and Alfred H. Brooks, geologists, and E. C. Barnard, W. J. Peters, W. S. Post, and Robert Muldrow, topographers.

In addition to these assignments, Messrs. W. C. Mendenhall and F. C. Schrader, geologists, were, upon request of the War Department, detailed to the military parties under Captains Glenn and Abercrombie, respectively.

Upon reaching Skagway two parties were detached, one in charge of Mr. Barnard and the other in charge of Mr. Peters. These parties, organized under the general direction of Mr. Barnard, successfully crossed the White Pass. They were to descend the Yukon and remain together until the mouth of the White River was reached, at which point the Peters party, with Mr. Alfred H. Brooks as geologist, was to enter upon a special field of work—the exploration of the White and Tanana river systems. The Barnard party was to proceed to the Klondike region for the purpose of making a topographic survey of the district adjacent to the eastern boundary of Alaska, the one hundred and forty-first meridian. It was planned to extend the surveys westward from the Yukon between the sixty-fourth and sixty-fifth parallels of latitude and to include the Fortymile district. The map to be made by Mr. Barnard's party was designed to serve as a basis for a careful geologic investigation of the region. The topographic work in this locality was to be on the scale of about 4 miles to the inch, and, in addition, it was proposed to map on the scale of 1 mile to the inch a small area including and adjacent to the new military post on the Yukon.

Messrs. Muldrow and Post were attached to parties under the direction of Messrs. Eldridge and Spurr, geologists, respectively. After parting from the Barnard and Peters parties at Skagway, Messrs. Eldridge and Spurr with their associates continued in the *Wheeling* to Cook Inlet, from which point they were to proceed up the Sushitna to about latitude 63° 40′, where several forks of the river combine. At this point the Eldridge party, with Mr. Muldrow as topographer, was to commence the exploration of the northeast portion of the Sushitna drainage basin, and, if possible, to close on Mr. Peters's survey down the Tanana. The other party, under Mr. Spurr, with Mr. Post as topographer, was to proceed westward across the divide between the Sushitna and the Kuskokwim for the purpose of surveying the head waters of the Kuskokwim and of determining the navigability of that stream by descending to the usual portage to the Lower Yukon.

All the parties expected to rendezvous at St. Michael by September 15, but the contingencies of exploration in remote regions could not be accurately foreseen and the chiefs of parties were at liberty to pursue such homeward routes as might seem most favorable under the conditions existing in the autumn. The Barnard and Peters parties descended the Yukon and returned from St. Michael; the Eldridge party was forced to return to Cook Inlet and thence to Seattle; and the Spurr party, on arriving at the mouth of the Kuskokwim, found opportunity for more extended exploration, and returned along the coast to Katmai, where it was picked up by the Alaska Commercial Company's steamer *Dora*.

The energy with which these parties pursued the explorations and surveys assigned them has been characteristic of American explorers, but is none the less creditable to these men. The methods with which they determined the positions and topography of their routes of travel, and the accuracy with which they observed the geologic and natural-history features of the country traversed, combine to render the results far more valuable than has usually been the case under similar circumstances. The reports which follow set forth briefly the principal results of their observations, giving in untechnical language useful information with reference to the geography, geology, mineral resources, animals, vegetation, climate, and population of the districts explored. All statements have been condensed.

To supplement the original information comprised in these several reports a compilation of all available authentic data has been made and is included in the second part of this publication. This second part relates to the whole of Alaska, which is divided into geographic provinces, and each province is described separately. Finally, a series of condensed tables of important information has been added.

The work of 1898 increased much the definite knowledge of Alaska which had been obtained by explorations scattered over the preceding years. The map of that portion of Alaska lying south of the Yukon has been almost completely reconstructed. Rivers previously known have been for the first time accurately surveyed, and many new lakes and rivers have been discovered. The mountain systems have been traced out, and magnificent ranges 12,000 to 20,000 feet in altitude have been found where previously the maps presented blanks. The source of the Kuskokwim has been found far distant from where it was supposed to be, in high mountains, where a swampy plain had previously been believed to exist. The physiography of southern Alaska has been independently studied and worked out by each party, and there is substantial agreement in all the principal incidents of interpretation. The important question of general glaciation has received special attention. The geologic formations and the distribution of coal-bearing and known gold-bearing rocks are broadly determined. Much valuable information has been accumulated in regard to the distribution of timber and game, with possibilities of agriculture or of stock raising, and in regard to feasible routes for pack trails, wagon roads, or railways, by which the country may be traversed or the interior reached.

The present report has been prepared in accordance with the special act of Congress, to accompany the maps of the several routes of exploration and the revised general map of Alaska. It has been written by the several geologists and topographers of the expeditions, and the whole has been edited by Mr. Spurr. Fuller discussion of the geology and physical geography of the regions visited by the different parties, with details of scientific and economic interest, will be presented in the Twentieth Annual Report of the Survey.

PART I.—SPECIAL REPORTS OF EXPEDITIONS.

REPORT OF THE SUSHITNA EXPEDITION.[1]

By G. H. ELDRIDGE and ROBERT MULDROW.

GENERAL TOPOGRAPHIC FEATURES OF THE ROUTE.

Cook Inlet is a structural basin of vast size, open to the North Pacific at its southern end. At present the sea occupies about half the total area, the remaining portion having been gradually filled and elevated until it now forms a broad valley 75 to 100 miles wide by 150 to 175 miles long. The inclosing mountain ranges have an intricate and rugged topography and an approximate average height of 8,000 to 10,000 feet, but they are sharply saw-toothed and relieved by numerous peaks 12,000 to 20,000 feet in altitude. The loftiest and most rugged mountains are those constituting the Sushitna-Tanana divide; they include the highest peak on the North American continent—Mount McKinley, 20,464 feet in elevation—and may be called the Alaskan Mountains. West of Mount McKinley, in the same range, are two peaks closely approximating 16,000 feet. The ranges which lie west of Cook Inlet and the Sushitna Valley resemble the Alaskan Mountains in ruggedness, and include a number of lofty peaks, of which the volcanoes Redoubt and Iliamna, 11,000 and 12,068 feet high respectively, are the most interesting. East of the Sushitna Valley and Cook Inlet, also, the mountain ranges have great ruggedness, and there are many points but little lower than those in the Alaskan Mountains. To the range north of the Kenai Peninsula the name Talkeetna may be applied. In all these ranges the crest line is saw-toothed, while the slopes are cut by gorges 4,000 to 10,000 feet deep, with precipitous walls, and their upper courses glacier-filled. At the head of Cook Inlet and west of the mouth of the Sushitna River lies Mount Sushitna. This peak is 4,280 feet high, forming the southern extremity of a low ridge that is cut by the Yentna, the chief western tributary of the Sushitna, a short distance above its mouth.

The vast watershed inclosed by all these mountains is drained by the Sushitna river system. What is locally regarded as the main branch of this stream rises far in the interior, in the comparatively low country between the mountains of the St. Elias and Alaskan systems, and has a course very irregular but in the main southwest. About 80 miles from the inlet it receives the Chulitna, and from this point the river has an almost due south course. The Chulitna has

---

[1] See map No. 2, in accompanying envelope.

many forks rising in the Alaskan Mountains, some of them originating in the canyons of Mount McKinley itself. Both the main river and the Chulitna carry heavy volumes of water, each stream averaging perhaps one-fourth mile in width. A mile below the Chulitna the Sushitna receives from the northeast the Talkeetna, a tributary of secondary size rising in the Talkeetna Mountains, and 20 miles above the mouth of the Sushitna the Yentna enters from the northwest. The last-named stream rises in the mountains forming the divide between the Sushitna and the Kuskokwim, and is approximately 150 miles long. Data relating to the region drained by the Yentna may be found in the accompanying report by Messrs. Spurr and Post (p. 28) All three of the great tributaries of the Sushitna carry vast amounts of sediment, derived from glaciers and from the banks, which are constantly wearing away. Their currents are between 4 and 5 miles an hour, and their main channels are deep.

The valley of the main Sushitna below its confluence with the Chulitna merges with that of the Yentna and forms a gently undulating tract of country, 100 to 125 miles broad, which rises gradually from 4 or 5 feet above high tide at the mouth of the river to 300 to 400 feet at the border of the foothills. From the summit of Mount Sushitna the valley appears to be well timbered with poplar, spruce, and birch, the latter on ridges and other elevated portions. Meadow and swamp land is freely interspersed with the timbered areas, and lakes form a conspicuous feature. At the periphery of the valley the country is generally high and rolling, in some localities forming foothills to the adjacent ranges, while here and there the general valley itself is cut by low yet conspicuous ridges, some of igneous rock, some of specially heavy gravel deposits, and, rarely, some of sedimentary rocks.

At the mouth of the Sushitna is a large delta that is traversed by three or four channels of considerable size, of which the westernmost is used by Indians and traders for access to the river, since it is deeper and shorter and safer of approach than are the others. The delta above the general tide level is a vast body of marsh land, relieved along the channels by fringes of alder and poplar and in the upper portion by spruce. As the distance up the river increases, the timber, especially spruce, grows thicker. Between the delta and the mouth of the Chulitna the Sushitna maintains a width of one-half to 2 miles, and is for the greater portion of the distance studded with islands, though there are occasional stretches where the stream flows through a single broad and deep channel. The stage of the water causes marked variation in the relative proportion of islands and bars, thus seriously affecting the ease with which the river is ascended, since, on account of the current, the greater portion of the distance has to be made by towing, either in the stream or along the main shores. Minor channels, however, frequently enable one to avoid the swifter currents. The main channel is generally well defined and of considerable depth, sufficient, it is believed, for the passage at all times of light-draft stern-wheel steamers. The banks of the river in the delta region are of sand, and rise but 5 or 6 feet above ordinary water level. With an occasional exception it is not until a point a mile or two above the Yentna is reached that the gravel banks, so common along the river above, become a pronounced feature. From this point, however, these banks continue quite to the foothills, varying in height from 25 to 200 feet. There are usually no bottom lands, in the sense in which the term is accepted in the United States, along either the main river or its tributaries.

From 5 to 10 miles above the mouth of the Chulitna the character of the main Sushitna Valley changes; it now lies in the foothills, and a little farther up is inclosed between ridges 3,000 to 4,000 feet high, which separate it on the southeast from the Talkeetna and on the northwest from the Chulitna. The stream itself runs in a picturesque gorge 400 to 500 feet deep, which has been cut in the bottom of an earlier valley. Forty-five miles above the mouth of the Chulitna, falls and rapids are reported in the main river, which prevent boating both upstream and downstream. However, for a distance of about 25 miles a portage may be made over the highlands on the northwest side of the river, and boats may then be again utilized for transportation of supplies nearly to the great glaciers at the head of the stream. The current in the upper river is much swifter than in the lower.

The ancient valley of the Sushitna, referred to above, is nearly closed at its lower end, 10 miles above the Chulitna; it broadens to 6 or 8 miles in the vicinity of Indian Creek, 25 miles farther up, and maintains this width in a general way as far as the great bend in the river 50 miles above the Chulitna. Beyond this it is said to further broaden and to take the character of an open highland country, with mountains here and there about its periphery. Although this early valley of the Sushitna shows evidence of having once been well worn down, nearly to base-level, it has since been deeply cut by mountain torrents and its floor has been rendered uneven by erosion of the underlying highly folded slates, so that the region is one of hills and dales beautified by growths of spruce and birch and interspersed with open grassy or moss-covered parks and lakes of great picturesqueness. The timber line in these mountain valleys reaches as high as 3,000 feet above sea level; above this the alder growth extends for 500 or 600 feet, and is succeeded finally by moss-covered slopes or bare rocks.

The general valley of the Chulitna was observed from the range separating it from the Sushitna River at a point opposite the mouth of Indian Creek, the distance between the streams here being about 15 miles. The course of the main Chulitna is a little west of south. It receives numerous large tributaries, glacial and otherwise, from the mountains to the west, while from the east there enter two important branches, fed by torrents that flow from icy amphitheaters high in the mountains on this side. The main valley lies directly at the base of Mount McKinley and the peaks northeast of it. It is well timbered and watered, and there appear to be hundreds of acres of meadow and grass lands similar to those in the upper portion of the Sushitna. At the head the Chulitna has several prominent forks, which rise far back in the range, some leading to passes less than 4,000 feet in altitude. Two of these forks were ascended last season, and the passes at their heads crossed, by independent parties from the Geological Survey and the Army. The Survey party crossed at the head of the easternmost fork, finding there two passes to the waters of the Tanana, about a mile and a half apart, one about 3,700 feet in altitude, the other 4,200 feet. The lower pass lies east of the other, with an approach of gentle grade on both sides. In the immediate vicinity of these are two other passes, one leading from what is probably an upper fork of the Sushitna, the other from a tributary of the Chulitna next west of that ascended by the Survey party. The latter pass is the lowest of the four and bears a small lake on its summit; it is probably about 3,500 feet in elevation and of easy approach. The Army party, taken from a detachment of the Fourteenth Infantry, under Captain Glenn, and consisting of Sergeant Yanert and a private, under the pilotage of an Indian took what is possibly the main tributary of the Chulitna and crossed the range at a point perhaps 10 miles west of the Survey party's route by a pass estimated at but 2,700 feet elevation and more direct. This pass, or the valley leading north from it, the Survey party saw on its journey toward the Tanana. It is probable that there are other passes to the east of the foregoing, and probable also to the west.

The tributary of the Tanana descended by the Survey party is probably the Cantwell River. Although the stream was not followed to the mouth, it is known to lie considerably to the west of that descended by the main Army party, which was identified as the Delta River. It is important in respect to size, receiving within the range many large tributaries, glacial and other. For a distance of 20 to 25 miles from its source the particular branch descended by the Survey party is confined to a narrow and tortuous gorge, when, after passing through a short box-canyon, it enters an enormous NE.-SW. valley, broad, well timbered, and dotted with lakes. This valley is drained by two great streams from opposite directions, which in their forks have left a high triangular-shaped mountain mass, each stream having carved for itself a deep canyon through the inclosing ridge on the northwest. Into the western of these streams flows the tributary descended by the Survey party. It is this western stream also which was descended by Sergeant Yanert, of the Glenn party, the pass at the head being reported low and easy, with a distance between timber of but 3 or 4 miles. Both the east and the west forks carry heavy sediments, derived from glaciers.

About 40 miles below the confluence of the two forks just described, for most of which distance the stream flows through a gorge with lofty mountains on either side, there enters another great tributary from the east, occupying a broad open valley not less than 50 miles in length and of the same general appearance as the valleys of the forks above. This lower fork is also a glacier-fed stream, and in size is about equal to that descended by the Survey party. About 15 miles below the latter confluence the river passes out of the mountain valley through a sharp canyon, apparently 8 or 10 miles in length, through which it was believed the open valley of the Tanana could be seen.

GEOLOGY.

FORMATIONS

The region traversed by the Survey party presents for examination a half-dozen formations and a structure broadly simple yet complex in detail. The formations include granite, which is perhaps in part basal; schists and slates, chloritic and other varieties; a series of conglomerates, coarse sandstones, and shales, with coal seams, belonging to the Kenai series; and glacial drift—gravels, sands, and clays or muds. The ages of the formations are undetermined, except the Kenai, which has been found to be Eocene or Oligocene.

Granite.—This is apparently of the same nature as that found elsewhere in Alaska. It is bright gray, moderately coarse in texture, and is either massive or of a heavy gneissic structure. Its chief components are feldspar, quartz, and biotite, with occasional hornblende.

The greatest body encountered was that of Mount Sushitna, whose entire mass above an altitude of 1,200 feet is of this rock; below this altitude no outcrops were seen. From the peak granite appears to form the core of a ridge which extends northwestward. A second locality is a small faulted area on the south side of the main fork of the Sushitna, about 18 miles above the mouth of the Chulitna. The granite here has a prominent gneissoid structure. A fault trending NW.–SE., and with a throw of possibly 1,000 feet, has uplifted the granite on the northeast and brought it against slates on the southwest. To the northeast the granite rapidly passes beneath the slates which constitute the succeeding formation. A third granite mass is exposed a short distance above the last locality, on the opposite side of the river, forming the core of the ridge between the Chulitna and the Sushitna and extending, with occasional interruptions, nearly to the head of Indian Creek. At the base of the ridge, on the southeastern side, it is fringed by the quartzites and slates of the period next younger in the field explored. Small remnants of the latter rocks are also to be found at several points along the crest of this ridge, and locally the series may extend quite over the summit. Granite also occurs on some of the tributaries of the Chulitna, but in comparatively small bodies; it was also found in isolated patches north of the divide.

Sushitna slate series.—Slates constitute one of the most important of the formations encountered. They are quartzitic in nature, varying in the coarseness of their material from fine to granular. The entire series has been extremely sheared and the sand grains have been crushed, producing thus the schistose or slaty structure. Mr. Whitman Cross, of the Geological Survey, examined the rock microscopically and found no grains referable to igneous rock, in spite of the impression from megascopic examination that the rocks were sheared eruptives. A feature of the formation in localities where great crumpling of the strata has taken place is the presence of quartz seams in large numbers, from a half inch to 2 feet thick, reticulating the exposed surfaces with considerable intricacy. Such seams often show mineralization with sulphides of iron, and it is believed that they constitute the source of much of the gold found in the bars of the Sushitna and elsewhere where the slate series is present. The thickness of these slates it was impossible to estimate, but it is believed to be several thousand feet. The series constitutes the main formation of the Alaskan Mountains, where these were examined. The first outcrop in ascending the main Sushitna occurs about 15 miles above the mouth of the Chulitna, and from this point the formation extends in an unbroken belt to a little above the falls, 55 miles beyond. The general trend of the series of slates east of the Sushitna River is parallel with that of the mountain range on that side—i. e., NNW.-SSE. West of the Sushitna its trend is like that of the Alaskan Mountains, changing to nearly E.-W. The general dip in both instances is away from the range axis.

North of the Sushitna-Tanana divide the slates are quite as fully developed as on the south, and again their prevailing dip is away from the mountains. They maintain the same features of composition, schistosity, cleavage, and quartz veinings, more or less mineralized, as south of the range. The total width of exposure of this terrane on both sides of the divide must be nearly 80 miles.

Cantwell conglomerate.—This is a series of conglomerates and coarse sandstones which was encountered in the banks of the Cantwell River 10 or 15 miles above the lower fork. The matrix in the conglomerate is quartz; the pebbles are dark slate. The relations of these beds to the formations of adjacent regions were not discovered.

Kenai series.—This embraces a succession of soft, light-gray sandstones and mud shales with interlaid coal seams and, according to reports of other observers, conglomerates. The age of the Kenai series has been determined to be upper Eocene. From the existence of this formation along the eastern shore of Cook Inlet, its presence from a point several miles southwest of Tyonek to the vicinity of Mount Sushitna, its recurrence on the Sushitna River, first about 20 miles from the mouth and again about 87 miles up, and still again on the Talkeetna, it seems possible that much of the Cook Inlet Basin, both above and below water, is underlain by the formation, its periphery being defined by the base of the surrounding ranges. Each of the above localities shows coal seams, and may therefore be of some importance in the future. The beds of the formation are rarely horizontal; in some localities they are inclined at as high an angle as 45°, but as a rule their undulations are more gentle.

Recent deposits.—The recent deposits of the Sushitna Valley and adjacent shores of the inlet are gravels, sands, and clays, laid down in two distinct periods. Belonging to the earlier is a blue-gray clay locally rich in small bowlders of materials derived from the encircling ranges—granite, slate, and the various eruptives—together with coal derived from the Kenai formation. In the later period were laid down, unconformably upon the foregoing, coarse, loosely cemented gravels having a sand matrix which in some instances so prevailed that the deposit became a pure but soft and friable sandstone. This latter series of gravels shows a varying thickness up to 200 or 300 feet; the average thickness of the lower blue clay formation could not, however, be determined, as its base usually lay below the water level, but 30 to 40 feet have been observed in some localities.

Eruptives.—Rocks of this class occur at various points in the Sushitna and Cantwell valleys and their adjoining mountain ranges.

STRUCTURE.

The structural features of the Sushitna Valley and its inclosing ranges could be gathered only so far as the route of travel and the allotted time permitted. In general, however, the valley appeared to be a syncline and the adjoining mountains anticlines, modified by local folds of secondary nature. The Talkeetna and Tordrillo ranges were not visited and may possibly be far more complex than this. The Alaskan Mountains, where crossed, are unquestionably of this structure; here the slates which enter so largely into its composition are thrown into a lofty anticline, the steeper side to the south, the axis ENE.-WSW. In the transverse section of the range many minor secondary folds were encountered, affecting seriously the local strikes and dips of beds.

As an instance of secondary folding, the ridge between the Sushitna and the Chulitna may be taken. It is distinctly anticlinal in structure, with a trend NNE.-SSW., the granite core being fringed with slates. To the south it rises gradually from the general valley of the

Sushitna, and to the north it sinks beneath the Upper Chulitna Valley. North of the divide secondary folding was again a feature at several points, notably in the vicinity of the confluence of the upper forks.

MINERAL RESOURCES.

The mineral resources of the region traversed, as at present known, are gold and coal.

Gold.—The gold thus far found is all in placers. The bars of the Sushitna River afforded a few fine colors wherever a pan was taken, but in no instance was the quantity of economic importance. A still smaller amount of gold was found in the younger gravels in the banks of the Sushitna, and again in the same beds along the shores of Cook Inlet. In the latter locality attempts have been made to wash the gravels, but apparently without success. In the torrential streams which feed the Upper Sushitna coarser gold was found in promising quantity, especially at one or two prospects in a run entering the river from the east a few miles below the mouth of Indian Creek. The gold thus found is evidently derived from the quartz seams which so intricately reticulate the schist series in the localities where special crumpling of the strata has taken place. The seams are in many instances charged with pyrite, some of which, on assay, has been found slightly auriferous, yet none of the quartz panned showed gold.

Gold was found again in placers on the Chinaldna, a tributary of the Talkeetna, in the same belt of schists from which it was probably derived on the Sushitna. It is reported that the slates of the Upper Sushitna resemble those in the vicinity of Turnagain Arm, in the streams cutting which very profitable placers have been worked.

North of the Sushitna-Tanana divide prospecting was not attempted, but the presence of the slates, together with the mineralized quartz seams, argues in favor of the presence of gold.

Coal.—The coal of Cook Inlet and the Sushitna drainage system occurs in the Kenai formation. On the route of the Survey party three areas of outcrop were encountered: one at Tyonek, on the west shore of Cook Inlet; a second bordering the Sushitna 20 miles above its mouth, and a third on the main fork of the Sushitna 87 miles above its mouth. The Tyonek field is the easiest of access, and its outcrops have for some time afforded coal for use in a small local steamer and for domestic purposes at the agency of the Alaska Commercial Company at this point. The area of this field was not investigated, but from independent accounts by prospectors and Indians it is inferred that it extends for several miles inland and at least as far north as the Theodore River; outcrops are reported on this stream and on the Beluga and the Chulitna to the south of it. This would make a length for the field on the strike of approximately 30 miles, with a width as shown at the beach of about 4 miles. The strata of this field, as exposed along the shores of the inlet, dip about 35° SE. The seams vary in thickness from a few inches to 16 feet, interrupted, however, in their solidity by frequent clay partings and layers of coal of lower grade than the average.

The outcrop of the coal measures of the Kenai, 20 miles up the Sushitna, lies along the east bank of the stream just below the Yentna. Only one or two narrow seams of coal were found, however, hardly more than indicating the presence of the measures. What the field might develop could be determined only by boring or other deep prospecting.

The third field of coal extends along the main river from a point 5 or 6 miles above the mouth of the Chulitna to one 8 or 10 miles above. The strata of the Kenai here form bluffs 100 to 300 feet high. A number of coal seams appear on both sides of the river, but none over 6 feet thick were observed.

North of the divide, on the lowest tributary of the Cantwell reached—that from which the party retraced their steps—there is an area of strata which resemble the Kenai formation and which carry a few very thin coal seams. The extent of the area was not determined, but from outcrops at a distance it seemed moderately large.

The coal of the foregoing fields is all of the same nature, a very low-grade lignite. In appearance it is often hardly more than a compressed mass of carbonized wood, in which it is sometimes possible to pull from a long stem slivers like those split from a natural tree-trunk. Stumps are frequently found in the beds, standing vertical to the layers. The color of the coal is black to brown, with a brown streak. Among the first impressions one gains on seeing these coal beds is a sense of their youth, and it is questionable if a younger example of the mineral can be found anywhere except in peat bogs in transition to coal. The following analyses illustrate the character of the coal:

Analyses of coal from the vicinity of Tyonek.

	No. 1.	No. 2.	No. 3.	No. 4.
Moisture....................	5.41	9.07	9.47	9.44
Volatile matter..............	65.13	49.41	53.53	48.75
Fixed carbon................	27.60	30.84	31.66	33.56
Ash.........................	1.86	10.68	5.34	8.25
Total..................	100.00	100.00	100.00	100.00
Sulphur.....................	.26	.41	.36	.49
Coke........................	none	none	none	none

No. 1. Portion of a vein crossing beach 4 miles west of Tyonek. Wood coal. Selected.
No. 2. Portion of a vein crossing beach 3¾ miles west of Tyonek. Coal. From best portions of three or four different veins.

No. 3. Portion of a vein crossing beach 2¼ miles west of Tyonek, the first west of the village. Coal. Representing a layer 1½ feet thick in a 12-foot vein.
No. 4. Portion of a vein 6 miles west of Tyonek, but from a pile at Tyonek stored for use on the small steamer *Perry*, plying on the waters of Cook Inlet.

For comparison there are added two analyses of the coal at Kachemak Bay, which is of the same formation as the coals herein discussed.

Analyses of coal from Kachemak Bay.

	Per cent.	Per cent.
Moisture	12.64	11.72
Volatile matter not moisture	43.36	46.50
Coke	37.14	34.64
Ash	6.86	7.14
Total	100.00	100.00

POSSIBILITIES OF AGRICULTURE.

Besides the mineral resources of the region under discussion, there are possibilities for extensive agricultural interests. In the Sushitna Valley, which from its position near the coast would be more adapted climatically for agricultural pursuits than the interior, native grasses—the blue-stem of the northern United States and others—grow profusely in many localities. There are rich meadows for native hay, and among the heavier plants the lupines are conspicuous. At Tyonek rye and oats have grown to full heads the last season, the grains having been dropped along the gravelly beach by prospectors early in May; here also, and at the Sushitna Station, the agents of the Alaska Commercial Company and the Indians raise annually excellent Irish potatoes, peas, turnips, beets, lettuce, and radishes. In the wilds of the valleys and mountain sides berries abound, including cranberries (high and low bush), the salmonberry (a berry resembling a dewberry in size and shape), blueberries, mossberries, bearberries, and currants, almost all of delicious flavor. The soils of the valleys are rich in loam and decayed vegetable matter, extending to depths of 4 to 10 feet. Marshes and swamps are susceptible to drainage, while the higher timbered areas are dry. Although the season as a whole is limited in length, it is to be borne in mind that by reason of the high altitude the summer days are very long and the rapidity of growth is marvelous.

CLIMATE.

The following tables will indicate the climatic conditions of the region traversed.

REPORT OF THE SUSHITNA EXPEDITION. 25

Temperature and weather observations in the Sushitna Basin in 1898.

Date.	Place.	Mean.	Maximum.	Minimum.	Range.	Remarks on weather, by days.
May 11-14	Mouth Sushitna River	45.5	55	39	16	⁶2 cloudy, 1 fair, 1 light rain.
May 15-21	Do	46.3	54	43	11	3 cloudy, 4 clear.
May 22-28	Mouth Yentna River	51.0	59	45	14	2 clear, 4 cloudy, 1 rain.
May 28-June 1	45 miles N. of Cook Inlet	52.0	64	44	20	1 rain, 4 clear.
June 2-3						2 clear.
June 4-9	57 miles N. of Cook Inlet	56.5	65	49	16	1 clear, 5 cloudy.
June 10-16	65 miles N. of Cook Inlet	67.0	81	57	24	6 clear, 1 rain.
June 17-23	75 miles N. of Cook Inlet	59.0	69	48	21	2 showery, 2 clear, 3 cloudy.
June 24-30	90 miles N. of Cook Inlet	59.3	68	52	16	1 rain, 5 cloudy, 1 clear.
July 1-7	110 miles N. of Cook Inlet	56.2	67	50	17	2 rain, 2 cloudy, 3 clear.
July 8-16	¹Sushitna River, mouth of Indian Creek	63.6	84	51	33	3 rain, 2 cloudy, 4 clear.
July 17-22	²7 miles NE. of mouth of Indian Creek	58.7	64	54	10	4 rain, 2 cloudy.
July 23-25						1 smoky, 1 rain, 1 cloudy.
July 26-Aug. 3	³10 miles NE. of mouth of Indian Creek	53.7	61	47	14	8 rain, 1 cloudy.
August 4-12	⁴15 miles NE. of mouth of Indian Creek	55.4	64	45	19	4 rain, 5 cloudy and partly cloudy.
August 13-17	⁵18 miles NE. of mouth of Indian Creek	50.2	54	46	8	4 rain, 1 cloudy.
August 18-27	En route: Indian Creek nearly to Tanana	49.2	63	35	28	2 rain, 5 cloudy, 3 clear.
Aug. 28-Sep. 5	Return to Tyonek	49.5	57	43	14	7 rain, 2 clear.
Sept. 6-15	Tyonek	50.3	54	47	7	5 rain, 5 clear.
Sept. 16-24	Do	49.0	56	41	15	1 rain, 7 clear, 1 cloudy.

¹Elevation 700 feet. ²Elevation 1,900 feet. ³Elevation 2,000 feet. ⁴Elevation 2,100 feet. ⁵Elevation 2,500 feet. ⁶On cloudy days the mists rarely rose much above the foothills.

The precipitation in 1898, May to September, is said to have been by far the greatest within the memory of the oldest Indian. In 1897, the data for which have been furnished by Mr. W. G. Jack, a prospector, the precipitation is regarded as more nearly the average.

Weather conditions in the Sushitna Basin in 1897.

Date.	Place.	Weather.
April 2	Tyonek	Clear.
April 3	En route up Sushitna River	Do.
April 4	12 miles N. of Cook Inlet	Do.
April 5	En route up river	Do.
April 6	Sushitna Station, 20 miles up river	Cloudy.
April 7-9	En route up river	Do.
April 10	Do	Rain a. m.
April 11	} 97 miles up river	{ Snow and rain all day.
April 12-13		Do.
April 14		Cloudy.
April 15		Rain.
April 16	En route up river	Snow; clear.
April 17		Cloudy; cold.
April 18	Sushitna River, mouth Indian Creek	Clear.
April 19	Portage Creek	Do.
April 20-23		Clear.
April 24-25		Showers.
April 26-30	} Portage Creek to Devil Creek; portage	Clear.
May 1		Rain and snow.
May 2-6		Clear.
May 7-11	Devil Creek and vicinity, on Sushitna River	Do.
May 12		Snow, 3 inches.
May 13		Rain.
May 14-17	Do	Clear.
May 18		Cloudy; rain.
May 19	Vicinity of Devil Creek. River starts breaking up.	Clear and cold, ¾ inch ice.

Weather conditions in the Sushitna Basin in 1897—Continued.

Date.	Place.	Weather.
May 23-25		Clear.
May 26		Shower; clear.
May 27-28		Clear.
May 29-30	Vicinity of Devil Creek	Shower; clear.
May 31		Rain.
June 1		Cloudy.
June 2		Showers.
June 3	Started up river in boats	Clear.
June 4-5		Clear.
June 6		Shower; clear.
June 7		Cloudy.
June 8-30	En route	Clear, with occasional light showers. Lightning on 14th at Buckley Creek.
July 1-2		Clear.
July 3		Rain.
July 4	Independence Creek	Clear.
July 5		Cloudy; warm.
July 6		Rain.
July 7		Cloudy.
July 8		Rain.
July 9-10	En route	Clear and cool.
July 11-12		Rain.
July 13		Clear.
July 14		Cloudy.
July 15	Mouth Lake Fork	Cloudy and shower.
July 16		Clear.
July 17-26	Head of boating on 26th	Clear, with occasional showers each day.
July 27		Rain.
July 28	Reached head of river, 4 miles above boating. This below glaciers.	Clear.
July 29	Start back down river	Do.
July 30	Clepser Creek	Do.
July 31	Lake Fork	Do.
Aug. 1-5	Devil Creek	Clear, with occasional showers.
Aug. 6		Rain.
Aug. 7-10	Devil Creek to Portage Creek; portage.	Clear, with occasional showers.
Aug. 11	Sushitna River, mouth Portage Creek	Clear.
Aug. 12	Vicinity of Portage Creek. On 15th	Do.
Aug. 13-15	started down river	Cloudy.
Aug. 16	Sushitna Station, 20 miles N. of Cook Inlet	Do.
Aug. 17-18	On 18th mouth of river	Clear.
Aug. 19	En route southward	Do.
Aug. 20	Ladds Station	Do.
Aug. 21	Tyonek	Cloudy; rain.

ROUTES TO THE INTERIOR.

There are several routes from Cook Inlet to the interior of Alaska; one from the head of the Matanuska, by way of the Delta River, to the Tanana, explored by Captain Glenn and detail, United States Army; a second from the Sushitna Valley by way of the Yentna and Kuskokwim into the western interior, followed by Mr. Spurr, of the Geological Survey; and a third, explored by the party of the Survey under the writer, by way of the Sushitna and Cantwell rivers to the Tanana. In the vicinity of the latter route are several passes by which the Alaskan Mountains may be crossed, one of which was taken by a detail from the Glenn party—Sergeant Yanert and a private, accompanied by one or two Indians. The route followed by the writer lay along the western shore of Cook Inlet from Tyonek to the mouth of the Sushitna River, thence up the river to the mouth of Indian Creek—thus far, 150 miles, by canoe. From here an old and very obscure Indian trail was taken across the uplands east of Indian

Creek to the head of this stream, distant from the mouth about 20 miles. A pass of 3,700 feet elevation leads hence to the valley of the Upper Chulitna, the route first passing through a cove in the range and thence to the easternmost of the upper and larger forks of the stream; this fork, about 10 miles from the head, further divides into two, a conspicuous conical point marking the confluence. The western of the forks leads to the desired pass, although the trail first leads to the east of the point mentioned, passing over a high ridge and thence into the upper valley. In this portion of the valley there is a steady but gentle ascent to the eastern of the two passes. From the pass the route lay directly downstream for about 65 miles, nearly to the open valley of the Tanana.

In reference to the desirability of a portion of the foregoing route, it is quite possible that it would have been preferable to have ascended the Chulitna in canoes, for from our later observations the belief was acquired that it was feasible, notwithstanding information from Indians to the contrary. In any event the latter route is worth attempting, since there could be little loss of time even should it be necessary to turn back, and if that were not necessary, greater and easier progress would be made than by the route which was followed across country, for in the latter instance all supplies must be packed on the back. Moreover, with the canoes at the head of the Chulitna it would not be a very difficult task to pack them across the comparatively short interval (10 miles) to the waters of the Cantwell. It is also possible that the tributary ascended by Sergeant Yanert will prove the natural and more direct route to the waters of the Cantwell and so to the Tanana. Moreover, there may be other advantages by this route, such as the constant timber supply which exists on both sides of the mountains to within a very few miles of the divide. Conditions in this particular could not be worse than on the route followed by the Survey party, where with the exception of a single locality no timber occurs for a distance of 60 to 70 miles, even alder being scarce for long distances.

Magnetic variations, Sushitna River, 1898.

Lat. (N.)	Long. (W.)	Place.	Date.	Variation (E.)
° '	° '			°
61 19	150 38	Mouth Sushitna River.	May 12-15	27 15
61 35	150 27	Mouth Yentna River.	May 26, 9:45 a.m.	27 20
61 54	150 07	Sushitna River	June 3, 4:30 p.m.	27 50
62 20	150 10	Forks Sushitna River.	June 26, 4:30 p.m.	29 30
62 49	149 39	Sushitna River mouth of Indian Creek.	July 5, 4:33 p.m.	29 30

REPORT OF THE KUSKOKWIM EXPEDITION.[1]

By J. E. SPURR and W. S. POST.

ITINERARY.

The Kuskokwim expedition, as landed at Tyonek, consisted of J. E. Spurr, geologist and chief; W. S. Post, topographer; and A. E. Harrell, Oscar Rohn, George Hartman, and F. C. Hinckley, camp hands. The purpose of the expedition was to ascend the west branch of the Sushitna River and to cross over from its head waters to those of the Kuskokwim, then if possible to descend the Kuskokwim as far as the water route to the Yukon, then by way of this water route and the Lower Yukon to reach St. Michael, where steamboats could be found to transport the party back to Seattle or San Francisco. Since nearly all of this region was entirely unknown, we hardly knew what preparations to make, but all our supplies were taken with a view of meeting so far as possible any condition which might be encountered. We started out with three light cedar canoes, specially built in Peterboro, Ontario, and these proved excellent for all-round purposes. We arrived at Cook Inlet on the 26th of April—a rather unfortunate time, since it was too late for ice and snow traveling and too early for water travel, the rivers being not yet broken; moreover, we were delayed several days by heavy gales. On the 4th of May, the gales having abated, two canoes proceeded to the mouth of the Sushitna, arriving there on the 7th, while a surveying party proceeded along the shore to the same place. On account of the condition of the ice, we were obliged to camp on an island in the delta until the 20th of May, when we started upstream in our boats, paddling or pulling ourselves up by the bushes. We had supposed the ice to be already broken, but the real break-up occurred while we were ascending the river to Sushitna Station, and we had exciting times dodging the ice jams. At Sushitna Station we attempted to secure Indians as guides, but were unable to do so, the natives claiming that the river we wished to ascend was too rapid and dangerous at that time of the year; very few of them, indeed, had any knowledge of the route at all. We accordingly left without guides and entered the western branch of the river, known to the natives as the Katcheldat or Yentna.

Although the Yentna River is not very long, it proved so difficult of ascent that it was the 3d of July before we reached the spot where we began our portage to the Kuskokwim. In the meantime we had

---

[1] See maps Nos. 3, 4, and 5, in accompanying envelope.

slowly worked our way through a series of snag flats which alternate with short narrow canyons, and had met with many accidents. Our journey over the Tordrillo Mountains, which we found to form the divide between the Sushitna and the Kuskokwim, occupied in all nearly two weeks, as we had to portage around canyons on the smaller streams and climb over a pass about 4,400 feet high. However, we finally reached, on the other side of the divide, a rapid stream of considerable size, which we afterwards found to be the Kuskokwim. After running down this river toward the north a hundred miles or so we saw a few Indians, for the first time in nearly two months; and on the 1st of August we reached the old trading post known as Vinasale, where, however, we were disappointed in finding no provisions. After leaving this place we ran down to the trading post Kolmakof, but finding no provisions here we continued to near the mouth of the river, where, at Bethel, we found a Moravian mission and a trading post. Here our party was divided, Messrs. Hinckley, Madison, and Harrell crossing to the Yukon by the water route and thence to St. Michael, from which point they proceeded homeward; the remaining four of the party proceeded down Kuskokwim Bay and attempted the exploration of the Kanektok, a river hitherto unknown. The ascent of this river proved difficult and occupied us nearly two weeks, after which we were obliged to portage more than 20 miles across a high mountain pass, on the other side of which we found a large lake which is the chief source of the Togiak River. Running down this river, in a few days we reached Nushagak, by the route outlined on the map. At Nushagak we hired skin bidarkies and paddled across Bristol Bay to the Naknek River, and by way of this river and the lake in which it heads reached the native village of Savonoski, from which point a rapid portage of 60 miles across the high and bleak Katmai Pass took us to the Aleut village of Katmai. After considerable delay at this point, we were luckily picked up by the Alaska Commercial Company's boat *Dora*, and reached Seattle on the 11th of November.

TOPOGRAPHY.

Cook Inlet.—Cook Inlet passes through and behind the barrier ranges which confront the navigator in a nearly continuous line from British Columbia to Prince William Sound. The entrance capes are rugged, while farther in low wooded plains slope down from the high flanking ranges.

The characteristic feature of Cook Inlet drainages is rapid flow from high altitudes to the sea in short distances. The Sushitna waters debouch from mountain gorges onto a sloping plain of glacial drift and gravels, which extends inland from the mouth of the river 100 miles northwest and north. The immediate region around the mouth is low, and in the surrounding panorama of mountains the only near feature is the isolated Mount Sushitna. In the distance rise the volcanic peaks of the Chigmit Range; then farther northward the Belug Mountains, the Tordrillo Range, and the McKinley or Traleyka Range; and to the east the mountains of Turnagain Arm and the Kenai Peninsula.

Skwentna region.—A short distance up the Yentna from its mouth the low banks are replaced by gravel bluffs 150 feet high, which continue the entire distance to the base of the mountains, the Yentna River roughly maintaining the grade of the plain. The junction of the Yentna with the Skwentna is marked by the isolated Yenlo Mountain.

The Skwentna is varied in character by four short canyons, which alternate with the wider valleys confined by gravel bluffs. Eighty miles from Sushitna Station the base of the mountains is reached. Above this the river flows in a valley flanked by peaks varying from 4,000 to 7,000 feet in height, while torrential streams, some of which are glacial, enter on either side. The mountain slopes are rugged and difficult of ascent; timber disappears at an altitude of 2,500 feet, and topography like that of the higher Rocky Mountains appears in the heart of the range. Remnants of glaciers lie high on the northern sides of the mountains, while below may be traced ancient marine terraces, giving more rounded contours to the lower slopes.

In its extreme upper part the valley of the Skwentna bends sharply to the south and has its source in lofty mountain masses. Some distance below the head, however, a portage of 20 miles over the main divide reaches the Kuskokwim waters, which flow northward from the same mountains. The pass traversed by us is 4,400 feet high and is surrounded by picturesque mountain peaks; it has an east-west course and crosses the range at right angles, and although not the lowest pass it is the most practicable. To the north, curving like a horseshoe, lie the structural valleys of Happy Creek and Ptarmigan Valley. These valleys are topographically continuous, are 5 to 10 miles in width, and are about 3,500 feet in altitude where they meet.

Kuskokwim region.—The Kuskokwim at the point where we reached it is already a large river, occupying a deep mountain valley with untimbered peaks on either side. After receiving many tributaries it finally leaves the mountains and enters a great gravel plain, where it splits into small shallow channels. Sixty miles beyond its rapid course is arrested, at the flats; and, soon after, meeting the eastern fork, it becomes a wide and sluggish river.

Farther down the river enters mountains, and leaving these below Kolmakof, flows through the treeless tundra. Here the banks are low, though they often run back to hills of some height. After leaving the mountain valley below Kolmakof, the mountains near

Holy Cross Mission on the north side of the Yukon can be seen in the distance, and to the south the detached Kilbuck Mountains and the ranges south of Kwinhagamut.

Kanektok region.—The Kanektok near its mouth flows through the same tundra as the Lower Kuskokwim, but 30 miles inland it again meets the mountain front.

The ranges here are extensive but are separated by wide valleys, and the rounded summits at first encountered are replaced in the heart of the range by sharp peaks. At the head of the Kanektok we encountered the first of the large lakes which are among the most noticeable and important topographic features of southwestern Alaska. From a small stream running into this lake a series of short carries between small lakes brings one to the main portage, which leads to Togiak Lake. The pass which is crossed is 2,200 feet high, and the mountains around are from 3,000 to 6,000 feet in altitude.

Togiak region.—Togiak Lake is bordered by imposing mountains. Descending the Togiak River we found the valley to widen to a plain, and at the seacoast the mountains are mostly distant. The coast from Togiak to Nushagak is usually bordered by a cliff, while in all the bays there are flats running far out at low water.

Nushagak region.—The Nushagak River is the most important one draining into Bristol Bay. Its chief source is the large Tikchik Lake, but it has several important tributaries. In its lower course it runs through the same low land which stretches toward Iliamna Lake and southward past Naknek; its higher parts lie in a mountainous country. The largest lakes in Alaska—Iliamna, Clark, Naknek, and Becherof—all lie within a short radius of the Nushagak district.

Naknek region.—In proceeding up the Naknek River a lowland country is passed, which suddenly gives way to precipitous mountains when the lake is reached. These mountains are frequently isolated, although the central mass forms continuous chains for considerable distances. Glaciers are more numerous here than in the regions previously described, on account of greater precipitation near the coast.

POPULATION.

The native of the Sushitna is Indian, probably belonging to the class of Athapaskans, and resembling in a general way the Copper River natives and those of the Tanana and Upper Yukon. These Indians speak a language which is very limited in vocabulary and inflection; they are of medium stature, with generally intelligent features, and are by occupation fishermen and hunters. The Sushitna Indians have a village at Tyonek, and another at the Sushitna trading post, but on the Skwentna they have no permanent habitations, although they ascend this river in the spring as far as the mountains for the sake of hunting. Neither on the upper, torrential portion of the Kuskokwim are there any permanent habitations, the first natives encountered being a hundred miles or so down the river; these belong to the same general type as the Sushitnas, and are called Kolchane by the other inhabitants of the Kuskokwim district. They are a poor and scattered people, wandering continually from place to place. We saw not more than a hundred of them altogether. From Kolmanof down to Bering Sea is found a comparatively numerous population of Eskimos, who subsist almost entirely on the fish, especially salmon, which annually ascend the river. The entire number of these people is several thousand, and they have many small villages. From the Kuskokwim to Katmai the people also belong to the Eskimo stock and speak the same language, although in different dialects. Their number is not large, but one often meets with permanent villages.

CLIMATE.

The climate in the vicinity of Cook Inlet is extremely local. Heavy storms often hang over the inlet for weeks, while the mountains around are bathed in sunshine; and often this is reversed. From the end of April until the latter part of May the ice and snow were too soft for traveling, except sometimes at night. The main break-up of the ice on the Sushitna occurred on the 19th and 20th of May. From that time the weather grew warm with surprising rapidity. The rainfall from early spring until the middle of July was very moderate, the weather most of the time being clear and pleasant. The rapidly melting snows on the mountains, however, swelled the rivers and caused frequent floods. By the middle of July we were at a point on the Kuskokwim about 100 miles below the portage, and from this time until the latter part of August we experienced a very rainy season, showers falling nearly every day and continuous rains being frequent. During this period the days, when clear, were warm and pleasant and the nights just cool enough to be agreeable. About the middle of August the increasing length of the nights and the more frequent frosts began to diminish notably the energy of the mosquitoes. By the first of September the marked increase in coolness indicated the beginning of the autumn season.

During the ascent of the Kanektok River, in the latter part of August and the first part of September, we experienced tremendous rains which lasted night and day. After the middle of September, however, less rainfall was encountered, although for all the rest of the season we were continually annoyed by very violent gales. During the latter part of September and the early part of November severe frosts at night began to be frequent, although we were proceeding southward. The middle of November is about the average limit of river navigation in the neighborhood of Nushagak.

VEGETATION AND BIRDS.

All along the river bottoms of the Skwentna there is an abundant growth of dwarf timber, consisting in the lower flats of poplar and willow, while the drier land has abundant spruce and birch. Beneath the trees, and also on broad flats which are treeless, are abundant shrubs, grasses, and flowering plants. The alder grows everywhere, even on the sides of the steep hills. In the early part of July, on the high ground on the upper part of the Skwentna, broad open glades were found where the grass grew very thickly and as high as the waist. Berries of various kinds, ferns, and flowering plants were abundant, the vetch, Rocky Mountain bluebell, Rocky Mountain sunflower, white buttercup, fireweed, violet, and many other blossoms being found. Moss is everywhere abundant, but is not so thick as in more humid regions on the coast farther south. The higher part of the pass, between the Skwentna and the Kuskokwim, was above timber line and was bare, save for moss and stunted bushes.

On the Upper Kuskokwim the vegetation is much like that of the Skwentna, the species of trees noticed being the birch, the spruce, the balm of Gilead, the small-leafed poplar, the larch, the willow, and the alder. Below Kolmakof the timber disappears, save for a slight growth of small balm of Gilead and willow close to the river. On the tundra, which reaches from here to the coast, only thick moss and stunted bushes grow, with various marsh plants, and sometimes mushrooms. From the Kuskokwim to Katmai the country has in general no timber, the only growths of spruce met with being found on the small Egoushik River, which lies to the southwest of Nushagak.

The migratory birds return very early to Cook Inlet. The sparrows, the robins, the warblers, the swallows, and the thrushes were seen here during the early part of the month of May. By the end of May the birds had commenced nesting, and we frequently disturbed the wild geese, the Arctic tern, the ducks, and the gulls as we passed by. Along the Skwentna River we found sandpipers and other shore birds in plenty, with gulls and terns; redpolls were very common, and several species of grouse were constantly met with. From the alders on the river bank the startling "Whoo-pee" of the fly-catcher was constantly sounded. On the portage at the head of the Skwentna we saw a number of warblers, including the common yellow warbler, and two species of three-toed woodpeckers, which are common in all northern countries. The hawk owl and the goshawk were occasionally met with in the woods. On the very summit of the pass, which is about 4,400 feet high, we found very few birds; here, besides the ubiquitous redpoll, we occasionally came across a brood of ptarmigan, and once we saw two pretty Arctic finches living among the high rocks. As we approached the summit we heard the scream of a golden eagle, which had its aerie in a crag near by. The general bird life of the Kuskokwim is very nearly like that which has been noted for the Skwentna.

GAME AND FISH.

The Skwentna and the Kuskokwim both flow through what is in general a remarkably poor game country. During our whole trip along these rivers we saw only two moose and one bear; and, moreover, there were no signs of any great number. Small game was very scarce, for although grouse and ptarmigan were occasionally met with in the woods they could not be depended upon; and rabbits were almost absent, only one small individual being seen. The extremely scanty population of Indians on the Skwentna and Upper Kuskokwim shows how small the game supply must be. In an abandoned Indian camp at the head of the Kuskokwim, however, we found splendid horns of the mountain sheep, showing the presence of this animal in that region.

The mountains lying between the Kuskokwim and the Togiak form apparently better hunting grounds than the Tordrillo Range, the signs of bear being especially abundant. Near Cape Etolin, between Nushagak Bay and Bristol Bay, our natives killed two caribou, which were the only large game we saw between the Kuskokwim and the Naknek River. The Alaska Peninsula has apparently comparatively good hunting grounds, the bear in the vicinity of Katmai being very numerous; we also saw two moose in the neighborhood of Katmai Pass. On the whole, however, the entire population of the country we traversed subsists essentially upon fish, which are usually plentiful, especially salmon, which ascend all the rivers in large numbers annually. In some of the streams also, especially the Sushitna, the small greasy candlefish forms an important article in the diet of the natives.

GEOLOGY.

In the vicinity of Tyonek were found partially consolidated gravels and clays which are of Tertiary age; they contain beds of lignite. Above this series lie thick stratified gravels, with occasional bowlders, and these gravels form for the most part the bluffs along the shore, covering over a broad area most of the underlying rock, which shows only in occasional ridges cut by the streams or protruding above the surface of the gravel plateau. Above the station on the Sushitna is found a volcanic rock, basalt. A short distance above the mouth of the Yentna this river cuts through granite, which is probably the extension of Sushitna Mountain; and Yenlo Mountain, farther up, at the junction of the Yentna and the Skwentna, is probably a recently extinct volcano, since volcanic pumice is found near its base. The

Shell Hills, as shown by the rocks in the first canyon of the Skwentna, are of ancient basalt; and from these hills to near the portage across the Tordrillo Mountains the rocks ordinarily are old volcanics, the lavas alternating with tuffs, which are simply the consolidated coarse sand and mud once worn away from the volcanic rocks and afterwards hardened. On account of their age these volcanic rocks are altered in appearance, being of a greenish color, often black, sometimes suggesting limestones and sometimes sandstones. As a whole they are cut by occasional diorite and granite dikes. On both sides of the crest of the Tordrillo Mountains for several miles there are heavy black shales with indistinct plant remains, and these are cut by a broad dike of granite, which forms the axis of the range and sends out many smaller intrusions. On the Kuskokwim side of the mountains is found the same stratified gravel deposit as on the Sushitna side; this is generally level, but slopes gently away from the mountains and covers up most of the solid rocks beneath. A hundred miles or so from the mountains the river enters broad flats which are covered with a thick deposit of silt. These flats, like those of the Yukon and other Alaskan streams, are evidently the bottoms of ancient shallow lakes which have recently been drained. Proceeding from here down the Kuskokwim, one finds sedimentary rocks nearly continuously for hundreds of miles, as far as the Yukon portage. These consist of impure shales, limestones, sandstones, and occasionally conglomerates, all intimately interbedded. On the upper river, near the camp of July 29 (see map No. 3), Devonian fossils were found, and below Kolmakof probable Cretaceous fossils; but between these horizons there is evidently a gap. Through all these sedimentary rocks there are dikes of general granitic nature. In the region of Kolmakof and below there is an increase in the number of granitic dikes, and some schistose rocks are found, together with occasional volcanics. From this point down to the coast there is a continuous deposit of clay overlain by peat, which forms the foundation of the tundra. The mountains which lie between the Kanektok and the Togiak rivers contain the same sedimentary rocks as are found on the Kuskokwim in some places, together with many large intrusive bodies of syenite, granite, diorite, and some ancient lavas. From Togiak Lake to Nushagak there is found mostly the volcanic rock, basalt, and tuffs which have evidently been derived from the same rock. The hills in this region have the appearance of being ancient volcanoes. From Nushagak to Bristol Bay the high bluffs are entirely of gravel, but two separate gravel formations are distinguishable, the upper one level and the lower one slightly folded; both contain pebbles scratched by ice. These gravels reach to Naknek Lake, where volcanic rocks (andesite-basalt) are found, with dikes of syenite and granite. On the upper part of the lake a series of sedimentary rocks consisting of sandstones, shales, etc., occurs, and these rocks extend, with interruptions, as far as Katmai Point, and at several places they contain fossils which show their age to be Upper Jurassic. Along the axis of the range the Jurassic rocks are cut by a chain of volcanoes whose lava is an andesite-basalt. These volcanoes have probably been active in comparatively recent times, and hot springs and earthquakes are among the present phenomena.

Résumé.—The region from the mouth of the Skwentna to near the axis of the Tordrillo Mountains, also the whole region from the Togiak-Kanektok divide to Katmai, and the region between Kolmakof and the Yukon portage, are chiefly covered with volcanic rocks or with sedimentary rocks evidently derived from the volcanics (tuffs). The lavas, however, belong to different ages, only the line along the Alaska Peninsula (Aleutian Mountains), which probably extends as far as the Skwentna (Yenlo Mountain), appearing to have been recently active, although along this line there are other more ancient lavas. The region from Togiak to Nushagak shows no active volcanoes, but the old volcanic cones are very likely Tertiary in age.

Apart from the volcanic areas the district from the Tordrillo Mountains down the Kuskokwim to the Yukon portage consists of little-disturbed sedimentary rocks corresponding in general to the similar Paleozoic and Mesozoic rocks on the Yukon. The older schistose rocks of the Yukon, such as the Fortymile series and the Birch Creek series, do not appear anywhere in the region.

MINERAL RESOURCES.

Near Tyonek are found frequent seams of brown lignite, which has been sometimes used for steaming, but which in general is of a very low grade. On the Skwentna River below the junction of the Hayes River similar lignitic seams were found. Coaly seams, and even impure coal, occur on the Kuskokwim in the sedimentary rocks, especially in the vicinity of Kolmakof; but so far nothing of value is known. Heavy seams of lignitic coal are found on Nunivak Island and the adjacent mainland, these localities lying between the mouth of the Kuskokwim and that of the Yukon. Coal and oil have been reported on the coast northeast from Katmai.

On the Skwentna River the gravels almost always contain small quantities of gold, usually fine, although sometimes coarse grains are found, especially near the mountains. In a canyon on the Skwentna below the mouth of Happy Creek granitic dikes cut the basalts and tuffs and bring about some mineralization, shown by the presence of pyrite, copper pyrite, and galena near the dikes. Random samples show that this rock is sometimes a low-grade ore, the highest assay taken showing one-tenth ounce of gold and one-fourth ounce of silver, making a value of something over $2 to the ton. On the Kuskokwim drainage gold is found in gravels in the streams near the Tordrillo Mountains. Elsewhere on the Kuskokwim, however, the gravels derived from the purely sedimentary rocks are generally entirely barren of gold. In the region about Kolmakof, where there are more intrusive rocks and more folding, there is a little more mineralization also; and gold in small quantities, as well as cinnabar, the ore of mercury, has been reported. In the southern extension of these Kuskokwim Mountains a specimen of realgar and stibnite, the ores of arsenic and antimony, has been seen from the Kwiklimut River. From the Lower Kuskokwim to Katmai, also, the gravels in general contain no trace of gold, the volcanic region being apparently without much mineralization. On the whole, therefore, the country traversed does not show signs of great mineral wealth. The most favorable region is undoubtedly the Tordrillo range of mountains, which is very difficult of access. Possibly the best way of reaching these mountains is by Lake Clark.

LAND AND WATER ROUTES.

At Cook Inlet the harbors open throughout the year are Saldovia, Kachemak (Homer post-office), Kamishak, and Snug Harbor. From April to October Tyonek is open for specially piloted vessels of medium draft.

The mouth of the Sushitna is impassable for anything except flat-bottomed craft. From its mouth to its junction with the Yentna it is navigable for small boats, as is the Yentna for 40 miles to its junction with the Skwentna. The current is from 4 to 7 miles an hour. Shortly above the junction the Skwentna is torrential and can hardly be said to be navigable even for canoes. On the west side of the mountains the Kuskokwim is likewise torrential and entirely unnavigable as far as the Indian village shown on the maps. Below this village there is good steamboat navigation 600 miles to the sea. The current does not exceed 7 miles an hour at any point below this, and will average about 4 miles.

The Sushitna natives follow the Beluga River from the coast and then northward to the junction of the Yentua and the Skwentna across the gravel plateau. This route could be extended and the Tordrillo Mountains crossed at one of the low gaps to the gravel plateau on the west side, from which point a route could be laid out to the Tanana and thence to the Yukon. This route from Cook Inlet to the Yukon would be excellent for a wagon road or railway, there being no obstacles to overcome by engineering, nor any high mountains to cross.

A route long known and occasionally traveled, especially by natives, leads from the Kuskokwim above Kolmakof to Nushagak by way of the Holiknuk and the Nushagak rivers. The Holiknuk is said to have an extraordinarily crooked course in its lower part.

The so-called portage to the Yukon from the Kuskokwim is in reality a water route which leaves the Kuskokwim at the native village of Kalchagamut. The total length of the route is 66 miles, although the air-line distance between the rivers is only 20 miles. The country is all clay and gravel, and the highest bank crossed on the portages is 40 feet. The relative elevation of the Kuskokwim and Yukon rivers has not been determined, but enough has been seen to warrant the possibility of opening a water route. The current of the Kuskokwim being less than that of the Yukon, the presumption is that, if diverted, the Yukon would flow toward the Kuskokwim. The latter river is free of ice nearly two weeks earlier than the Yukon, and the lower Bering Sea is comparatively open while St. Michael is still blocked. If, therefore, supplies could be brought in by way of the Kuskokwim and thence across by the water route to the Yukon, there would be many advantages. The following table gives the saving in distance of the new route, the distances being taken from Unimak Pass.

Yukon route:	Miles.
Unimak Pass to St. Michael	720
St Michael to Talbigsak River	250
Total	970
Kuskokwim route:	
Unimak Pass to Goodnews Bay	360
Goodnews Bay to Kalchagamut	230
Kalchagamut to Talbigsak River	60
Total	650
Difference in favor of Kuskokwim route	320

The Togiak River is probably navigable for steamboats, and the Nushagak is likewise navigable for probably 90 miles. The Kvichak River, the outlet of Lake Iliamna, is not navigable for steamboats, but small boats can be towed up it. From Nushagak to Katmai two routes are used: one by way of Naknek River and Lake, and thence across the mountains to Katmai; the other by way of Igagik River and Becharof Lake to Cold Bay, and from these along the coast to Katmai.

Table of distances taken along route followed by the expedition from Tyonek to Katmai.

	Miles.
Tyonek	0
Mouth of Sushitna River	35
Sushitna Station	53
Junction Yentna and Sushitna	56
Junction Skwentna and Yentna	99
Junction Portage Creek and Skwentna	164
Summit of pass	179

REPORT OF THE KUSKOKWIM EXPEDITION. 39

	Miles.
Junction Styx River and Kuskokwim	189
Junction East Fork and Kuskokwim	296
Vinasale	393
Junction Chagavenapuk River	463
Junction Holiknuk River	508
Kolmakof Trading Station	637
Kalchagamut	706
Oknavigamut	716
Bethel	787
Warehouse	865
Kwinhagamut	880
Beginning of portage from Kanektok to Togiak	982
Togiak Lake	1,006
Mouth of Togiak River	1,061
Togiak	1,067
Head of Kululuk Bay	1,108
Mouth of Egoushik River	1,203
Nushagak	1,223
Naknek	1,302
Savonoski	1,376
Katmai	1,425

Magnetic variations,[1] *southwestern Alaska, 1898.*

Lat. (N.)	Long. (W.)	Place.	Date.	Variation. (E.)
° '	° '			° '
61 10	151 10	Tyonek	May 1	27 15
61 58	152 40	On Skwentna River	July 5, 9 a. m.	27 20
62 00	152 46	On Portage Creek	July 6, 1 p. m.	27 19
61 59	152 57	On Portage Creek	July 12, 8 p. m.	26 58
61 59	153 01	Near pass	July 14	26 29
62 00	153 04	Do	July 15, 8 p. m.	25 58
61 59	153 05	Do	July 16, 2 p. m.	25 45
61 31.5	160 42	Kuskokwim River	Aug. 7, 2 p m.	23 51
61 26	160 46	Do	Aug. 7, 7 p. m.	23 50
61 17	160 45	Do	Aug. 8, 2 p. m.	25 37
60 53.5	161 18	Do	Aug. 9, noon	20 22
60 47	161 52	Bethel	{ Aug. 10, noon Aug. 10, 6 p. m.	21 14 21 20
60 35	162 16	Kuskokwim Bay	Aug. 20, noon	20 44
60 09	162 15	Apokagamut	Aug. 22, noon	21 25
59 46	162 01	Kwinhagamut	Aug. 24, 11 a. m.	20 38
59 53	160 15	Kagati Lake	Sept. 8, 1 p. m.	21 14
59 48	159 59.5	On portage	Sept. 12, noon	22 01
59 07	159 28	Oallek Lake	Sept. 22, 6 p. m.	23 13
58 56	158 27	Nushagak	Oct. 2, 10 a. m.	25 02
58 48	156 35	Naknek Lake	Oct. 11, 5 p. m.	24 53
58 33.5	155 27	Savonoski	Oct. 13, 3 p. m.	23 56
58 04	154 58	Katmai	Oct. 23, 11 a. m.	24 33

[1] Observed with a transit reading to 1'. Results ± 5' about.

REPORT ON THE REGION BETWEEN RESURRECTION BAY AND THE TANANA RIVER.[1]

By W. C. MENDENHALL.

INTRODUCTION.

As geologist attached to Military Expedition No. 3, commanded by Capt. E. F. Glenn, I had opportunity during the last summer to examine geologically the shores about the western end of Prince William Sound and a belt of country extending from Resurrection Bay, on the eastern side of Kenai Peninsula, to the Tanana River at the mouth of the Delta River. Incidentally the accompanying maps, covering a route which lay almost wholly within hitherto unexplored territory, were prepared.

The trip across Kenai Peninsula was made very early in June, before the snow had entirely disappeared, and that from Turnagain Arm to Knik Arm late in the same month. Both of these were packing trips, each member of the party carrying his provisions and bedding, and gathering such scientific data as circumstances permitted.

The main expedition from Knik trading post to the Tanana River was begun on July 23, and the party returned to Knik on the 24th of September, having traveled about 675 miles by trail in two months. This trip, although hurried, was made under more favorable conditions for scientific work than the earlier shorter ones, since the pack train relieved the explorer of the embarrassing necessity of carrying on his own back food, blankets, and instruments.

The route lay up the Matanuska Valley nearly to its head, then north up Hicks Creek, across the head of Caribou, and out into the valley of Bubb Creek, one of the upper tributaries of Taxlina River. Here we found ourselves north of the coastal mountains and at the southern edge of a plateau basin with a level floor which stretched to the Alaskan Mountains, 100 miles by trail to the north. By the 21st of August we were on northward-flowing waters, which later proved to belong to the Delta River. This stream led us by an easy route through the Alaskan Range. A week later, when within the Tanana Valley and about 10 miles from the river itself, we turned back. The return journey was made more rapidly, and followed in the main the same course which we had established when outbound, until Bubb Creek was reached. Here we left our old trail to the west and entered Matanuska Valley at its head, picking up the old line again at the mouth of Hicks Creek. Seven days more of travel and we were back at salt water.

---

[1] See map No. 6, in accompanying envelope.

GEOGRAPHY AND TOPOGRAPHY.

COOK INLET AND PRINCE WILLIAM SOUND.

Prince William Sound, formerly called Chugach Gulf, and Cook Inlet are the two most important indentations of the Alaskan coast line west of the Alexander Archipelago. The former lies between the meridians of 146° and 149° west from Greenwich. It has a very irregular shore line, insuring excellent harbors, and a broad sea connection. Its narrow inland extensions are fiord-like, with deep water open all the year round, and safe anchorages. The interior, however, is not accessible from the sound—except at its eastern and western extremities, Port Valdez and Portage Bay—because of a high mountain barrier to the north.

Cook Inlet, separated from Prince William Sound by Kenai Peninsula, is about 200 miles long from the entrance at Cape Elizabeth to the head of Knik Arm, and contrasts in many ways with the more easterly bay. Its tides are very high at the head, the flood running in with a bore which is a serious menace to the safety of small craft. The precipitation along its shores is much less than in Prince William Sound, so that snow is never so deep and does not cover the ground so late in the spring; and because of the lighter snowfall, timber is more abundant and the timber line is higher. Several large streams enter the head of the inlet, whereas none of any consequence flow into the sound; and these streams carry quantities of sediment, which transforms the head of the inlet into a series of deltas and mud flats unfavorable for navigation. But the valleys of these rivers offer easy highways to the interior. Prince William Sound is open to navigation throughout the year, but Cook Inlet is closed above East Foreland for five months by ice. Its climate, however, during the summer months is very pleasant, and warm enough to permit of the growth of many hardy vegetables and cereals. Its shores present more favorable agricultural conditions than most other parts of Alaska.

GENERAL TOPOGRAPHY.

Kenai Peninsula is a rough mountain mass, with a very irregular coast line and a broad lowland on one side only—the northwest. In other directions its shores rise abruptly, often precipitously, from the ocean, but from Kachemak Bay to the lower part of Turnagain Arm a gravel-covered platform intervenes between the mountain backbone and the water of Cook Inlet. This platform varies from a few to several hundred feet above sea level, is gently rolling or flat-topped, and heavily timbered and moss-covered. Across it from the interior flow the largest rivers of the peninsula—the Kussilof, which drains Lake Tustumena, and the Kenai, which drains Lakes Sillokh and Kenai, and heads near the eastern shore of the peninsula, northwest of

Resurrection Bay. Other streams of importance are Chickaloon, Resurrection, and Sixmile creeks, flowing into Turnagain Arm, and that other Resurrection Creek which empties into the bay of the same name and which illustrates so well the confusion often resulting from prospectors' nomenclature.

Kenai Peninsula is connected with the mainland by an isthmus about 12 miles wide, separating the waters of Portage Bay from those of Turnagain Arm. Five miles of this isthmus is covered by a glacier, which flows down from the high summits to the south; the remainder is gravel delta, about 1 mile on the east and 6 miles on the west side.

Northward on the mainland the mountains of the peninsula continue, swinging eastward across the Copper River to their culmination in the St. Elias group. The Sushitna River empties into Cook Inlet from a course entirely to the west of these mountains, while the Matanuska Valley crosses them from the Copper River plateau, separating a minor group from the main mass to the east.

The northern limit of the St. Elias system is but little less definite than the southern. It breaks down abruptly at the head of the Matanuska River, and a broad, gently rolling, gravel-floored plateau stretches thence 75 miles northward to the foothills of the Alaskan Mountains. On this plateau, which is covered with a maze of lakes and marshes, the eastern tributaries of the Sushitna and the western branches of the Copper rise. Eastward the plateau basin is cut by the trench of the Copper River and limited by the Mount Wrangell group. Westward its surface becomes more diversified, until it merges with the hill country of the Middle Sushitna.

Approaching the Alaskan Mountains from the south across this interior plateau, the explorer crosses two preliminary groups of foothills before reaching the main range. By our route the first of these was encountered just after leaving Gakona River. It lies between the head waters of the Gakona and Chistochina, and averages only 1,000 or 1,500 feet higher than the valleys of these streams. Separating these hills from the next group to the north is the valley of the upper Chistochina, 10 or 20 miles in width, gravel-floored, and containing, like the greater plateau to the south, a large number of small lakes. Through this second range of hills, more regular and continuous than the first, broad gaps at about the level of the valleys are conspicuous.

The Delta River heads to the south of these hills in a chain of beautiful winding lakes, flows through a water gap east of Land Mark Gap, across another belt of open country, and then enters the Alaskan Mountains proper.

This great range stretches, with interruptions, from the St. Elias Mountains near the head of White River westward, along the divide between the Tanana on the north and the Copper and Sushitna rivers on the south, to the Mount McKinley group, west of the latter stream. The range is a series of lofty, isolated mountain masses rather than a definite and continuous chain. It is characterized by broad passes at an elevation of about 2,700 feet, and the groups between these passes reach heights of 10,000 to 15,000 feet. By the Delta River route the width of the range north and south is about 35 miles, and immediately after passing through it the traveler enters the broad valley of the Tanana River, which separates the Alaskan Mountains from the Ketchumstock and Tanana hills, farther to the north.

ROUTES.

An investigation in early April revealed the fact that between Portage Bay and Port Valdez there is no practicable route northward from Prince William Sound to the interior, that body of water being bounded in this direction by an extremely rough mountain barrier without passes and with culminating peaks 10,000 feet high. From Portage Bay, the most easterly extension of Prince William Sound waters, an easy winter trail exists across the isthmus to the head of Cook Inlet. During the summer this route is not used because at that time the waters of Cook Inlet are open and navigable for sea-going vessels.

From Resurrection Bay about halfway down the southeastern shore of Kenai Peninsula—Resurrection Bay itself being a harbor that is open winter as well as summer—there is easy access to the interior of the peninsula. A trail has been established up the valley of Salmon Creek, and thence across a low divide to Snow River, which empties into Lake Kenai. From Lake Kenai the Sunrise City mining district may be reached either by going up Trail Creek, which enters the lake near its eastern end, and thence crossing to the head of Bench Creek, a tributaty of the east fork of Sixmile, or by going up the valley of Quartz Creek, a tributary which enters Lake Kenai near its lower or western end, and crossing to the head of Canyon Creek. The latter of these routes is the shorter from Lake Kenai, but neither of them offers serious obstacles to the construction of either a pack trail or, if need ever should arise, a railroad line. The divides in both instances are low, standing at an elevation of something less than 1,500 feet above sea level, and very broad and flat. At present a part of this route from Resurrection Bay to Turnagain Arm is by water, there being no trail constructed around Lake Kenai. The building of a trail along the shores of this lake would be somewhat difficult, since the shores are steep and are subject to destructive snow-slides in spring. After reaching the head of the Sixmile drainage by either of these routes, the traveler finds fair trails already established by the miners at work on the waters of this stream.

From Juneau Creek, which enters Kenai River from the north, just below the outlet of the lake, a route is reported across the divide to the north into the basin of Resurrection Creek, thence down this creek to Hope City at its mouth. Before the trail down Sixmile Creek was established, pack trains with supplies for the miners on Canyon Creek went from Hope City up Resurrection Creek to Pass Creek near its head, and then climbed through the low divide to the head of Summit Creek, which enters Canyon Creek in the heart of the mining district.

From Turnagain Arm northwestward to Knik Arm at least two overland routes are available at present. One of these is by way of Indian Creek and is reported to be very short and to offer no serious obstacles. The other, which appears on the map (No. 6), is from the head of Turnagain Arm by way of the valley of Glacier Creek, and leads over a rather high divide—3,750 feet above sea level—to the upper waters of Yukla Creek. This stream enters Knik Arm almost due south from the North American Trading and Transportation Company's station.

The route from the head of Cook Inlet to the Tanana, which was examined last summer, while probably longer than the one by way of Valdez Inlet and Copper River, is perfectly feasible for the establishment of a trail or railroad, which would pass up the valley of the Matanuska to a 3,000-foot divide at its head. The approach to this divide, however, is at least 100 miles long, and gives ample distance for overcoming the elevation. After passing from the valley of the Matanuska to the interior plateau, no obstacles of importance are encountered until the foothills of the Alaskan Range, 75 miles to the north, are reached. Here a short climb of 400 or 500 feet out of Gakona River Valley must be made in order to reach the head waters of the Tanana drainage. Probably by swinging eastward or westward from this interior plateau other routes may be found down other branches of the Tanana which will possess special advantages, depending upon the point at which it is desired to reach the latter stream. Along practically the entire distance from Cook Inlet to the Tanana sufficient timber is found for furnishing ties and fuel, and the open character of the valleys and of the interior plateau reduces the danger of earth- or snow-slides to a minimum. It is scarcely necessary to add that over any route which permits the establishment of a railroad a pack trail can be built at comparatively small cost.

METHODS OF TRAVEL.

The Sunrise mining district may be reached previous to the 1st of May by the Portage Bay route within a distance of 40 miles, or by the Resurrection Bay route within a distance of 90 miles, from open water; before that date travel is wholly by sled or packing. After May 1 steamers reach the head of the inlet and give direct access to this district. The interior of Kenai Peninsula is also reached by way of Resurrection Bay in winter by sledding, while in the summer season it can be approached by this route or by way of Sunrise City, either with pack animals or on foot. Small boats may also be taken up the Kenai or Kussilof rivers by tracking, but this method is very laborious and slow.

At present the best methods of reaching the interior from the head of Cook Inlet are by sledding up the rivers in the winter months, and by the use of pack trains in the summer season. Pack animals will be able to live off the native grasses during June, July, August, and a part of September. Often all of the latter month may be relied upon on the coast side of the mountains, but north of this range freezing begins in August, and the grasses then rapidly lose their nutritive value. The Tanana River at the mouth of the Delta can be reached from Knik in a month of rapid traveling; but in order to insure the arrival of the stock in good condition thirty-five days at least should be estimated for the trip. Horses seem better adapted for this work than mules, because of considerable areas of soft ground which must be crossed; in these areas and in the mossy tracts the smaller feet of the mule are a decided disadvantage. Pack animals should be chosen which have been reared on the range and are accustomed to depending entirely upon grass for a living.

Heretofore supplies have been taken short distances up the Matanuska River in boats, but the stream is so full of shoals and so swift that tracking, which is the only possible way of making progress upstream, is too slow and is attended with too many possibilities of loss to be regarded as practicable.

GENERAL GEOLOGY.

SUNRISE SERIES.

About the western end of Prince William Sound, the northern part of Kenai Peninsula, and the adjacent mainland the rocks are dark slates and gray tufaceous sandstones or arkoses. They have been altered somewhat, developing a cleavage in the slates and a joining in the more massive beds. At least two systems of quartz veins occur in the harder rocks, usually very thin, and, so far as observed, never persisting across the boundary into the slates. Quartz occurs also in pockets, which may locally reach several feet in thickness, and sometimes at least are mineralized. The rocks contain a few thin diabase dikes and more numerous highly altered acid dikes, originally probably aplites. These latter in some instances carry gold, introduced probably at the time of the great metasomatic alteration to which they have been subjected.

Age.—No fossils have been found in these rocks, but from their relations to the Matanuska series, described below, it seems probable that they are pre-Cretaceous.

MATANUSKA SERIES.

Throughout the Matanuska and the upper part of Taxlina valleys the rocks, wherever examined, proved to be unaltered or but slightly altered sediments; shales—red, black, and buff—predominate, but some limestones, sandstones, and conglomerates occur. Of the latter, that forming Castle Mountain is by far the most imposing bed, measuring probably 1,000 feet in thickness. Bedded limestones were noted at but one point, and that the most northerly reached, on the head waters of Bubb Creek; here a shallow syncline brings a stratum of gray limestone 200 to 400 feet in thickness down to the hilltops. Beds of limestone concretions are sometimes found in the shales.

The strike of the series, although interrupted by many minor structures, is generally parallel to the mountan range and to the valley of the Matanuska River—i. e., about N. 70° E. Dips vary greatly, but are usually away from the coast, and steepest as the latter is approached. Many faults of unknown but probably slight throw, and light folds, make an accurate estimate of thickness with the data in hand impossible, but 6,000 feet is probably a safe minimum estimate. The slight evidence gathered favors the theory of an overlap of the Matanuska series upon the older Sunrise series to the south.

Age.—A few fossils collected at the base of the limestone bed mentioned above are pronounced by Mr. Stanton to be Lower Cretaceous. The relation of this bed to the rest of the Matanuska series indicates that the latter can not well be younger.

GREENSTONE SERIES.

Across the interior basin, in the first line of foothills of the Alaskan Range, a series of green schists, diabases, and augite-diorites is found. The schists are probably derived from the diabases in some instances at least, but are now highly altered and contain much secondary quartz, chiefly in veins. There is at present no evidence available as to their age, and so far as known they have no economic value.

TANANA SERIES.

Along the lower valley of the Delta River, through the heart of the Alaskan Range, the rocks are chiefly quartz-schists. Their alteration is so complete that except for a few narrow graphitic bands their original character would be in doubt; but this belt indicates their clastic origin. They have been intruded at several periods by both acid and basic dikes; they have highly developed schistosity, and carry two or more series of quartz veins. The older series has been much squeezed and broken, while the younger is one of the latest phenomena. Accompanying the quartz veins is a high degree of mineralization, sulphurets in variety and abundance occurring. Analyses of samples taken from these mineralized zones failed to show gold, and pannings of side tributaries whose gravels were derived entirely from the schists were likewise unproductive of results, although as much as a teaspoonful of sulphurets was caught in the pan.

Between the areas occupied by the greenstones and the schists is a narrow belt of rhyolites and derived fragmentary material.

KNOWN GOLD DISTRICTS.

Turnagain Arm.—Of the formations described above, the only ones known to carry gold are the Sunrise and the Matanuska series. The productive portion of the former, so far as now known, occupies a small portion of the northern end of Kenai Peninsula and a limited belt along the mainland north of Turnagain Arm. So far, within this district only placer diggings have been developed, although within the last season a few quartz claims have been staked. Whether or not they will prove to have sufficient value to justify development is a question that only the future can answer.

The placer values within the district are not high, ranging from $2 or $3 a day to the man to as high as $120 in exceptionally rich ground near the mouth of Mill Creek, one of the upper tributaries of Sixmile. So far the work has been confined entirely to sluicing and wingdamming, although hydraulic work will probably be done in the near future.

Matanuska Valley.—The rocks of the Lower Matanuska Valley are known to contain gold, but the region has not been systematically developed and no definite idea has been gathered as to the quantity. A quartz vein on Lower Chickaloon Creek is reported to have assayed $6 or $7 to the ton, and washings in the lower course of Schoonoven Creek have yielded values equivalent to $2 or $3 a day to the man. This gold probably has genetic connection with a series of diabase dikes which intrude the sediments of the valley in the neighborhood of Chickaloon Creek.

General gravel sheet.—Surrounding the northern end of Cook Inlet is a broad belt of lowland covered by gravels varying in depth from a few feet to a few hundred feet, which probably represent delta deposits at a period when the land stood much lower than it does at present. These gravels extend well inland up the various tributaries of Cook Inlet, and are again encountered across the divide at the head of Matanuska River in the interior plateau. They floor this plateau to unknown depths from the northern base of the Coast Range to the southern base of the Alaskan Range. They fill the valleys between the foothills of the latter, and are found again in full development on the head of the Delta River. North of the Alaskan Mountains morainal gravel is distributed as far as the Tanana.

This general sheet everywhere seems to carry small quantities of gold, and as practically all streams examined flow for at least a part of their courses through it, they yield colors (flakes of gold) to the prospector wherever he may pan. These colors are very puzzling, since it is impossible to tell, without a knowledge of the distribution of the gravel, whether they may have been derived from it or directly from rock in place; but the ordinary prospector, finding fine colors on the lower course of a river, naturally supposes that the gold has been derived from rock in place near the head of the stream, and plans accordingly. This supposition often proves to be entirely erroneous and leads to serious loss in individual cases. As a general rule it may be said that prospecting, to yield any reliable information as to the gold content of the country rock, should be conducted well up in the heads of the tributaries, and the miner should be certain that he is beyond the limit of the gravel sheet.

COAL.

The sediments of Matanuska Valley carry coal which, judged from the thin seams examined at one or two points, is of very fair steam-producing quality. Mr. Hicks, guide of the expedition, reports coal up Chickaloon Creek, and a bed 6 feet thick on a small stream, called Coal Creek, which enters the Matanuska opposite the mouth of the Chickaloon. North of the valley of the latter stream several dark streaks were noticed in the mountain side west of the valley, which probably represent outcrops of coal beds, since fragments of bright hard coal were found below these outcrops in the gullies. In the valley of Bubb Creek, which belongs to the Copper River drainage system, seams of coal a few inches thick were noted at a few points. Whether or not beds of sufficient thickness to prove even locally valuable occur in this part of the series can be determined only by further and more detailed exploration.

TIMBER AND GRASS.

On Kenai Peninsula the timber line stands at about 2,000 feet. Below this, spruce, birch, and several varieties of poplar clothe the slopes. The trees are small, occasionally reaching a diameter of 4 feet near the ground, but averaging probably 18 to 24 inches. The timber generally has no value aside from that of fuel, being wholly inferior to the heavier forests found farther south along the coast. Toward the interior from Cook Inlet the timber line gradually rises with the snow line, so that throughout the interior basin, which stands at an elevation of nearly 3,000 feet, scrubby spruce is found. A larger and better quality of spruce grows in thick forests along the lower courses of the Delta River and other tributaries of the Tanana.

Nutritious grasses grow abundantly in the birch groves of the Matanuska Valley, and coarser varieties fringe the shores of the lakes and ponds of the interior plateau. Considerable meadows are found along the valley of the Delta River, and nowhere was there serious trouble in finding plenty of grass for the animals of the pack train.

GAME.

In the high St. Elias Mountains on Kenai Peninsula and the mainland the white mountain sheep (*Ovis dalli*) is found in great numbers. It has as yet been hunted but little and is an important source of food for the prospector. This sheep is found also, but apparently in less abundance, in the Alaskan Range.

The moose is plentiful throughout the valleys of the entire region explored, but is very shy and difficult to obtain by the inexperienced hunter. Caribou are very plentiful in the foothills of both the Coast and Alaskan ranges. They select the hard, dry ground above timber line, seldom or never descending into the valleys, and were not seen at all in the broad interior basin. Although their distribution is thus somewhat limited, they are easy of approach, and, within the districts where they are found in such numbers, form an important addition to the explorer's food supply. Brown and black bear may be found in the mountainous districts everywhere, but are absent over the interior plateau. Fur-bearing animals occur in limited and constantly decreasing numbers; among the most important are the silver-gray, black, red, and cross fox, the wolverine, the otter, the beaver, and the gray wolf. Waterfowl in great numbers and variety throng the tidal marshes of the coast during the early spring and late fall, and are found during the summer season on the innumerable lakes of the interior plateau. Among the land game birds, ptarmigan and grouse are by far the most important, the former frequenting the untimbered uplands and the latter living in more or less abundance within the spruce and birch forests everywhere.

CLIMATE.

Along the coast the climate is remarkably mild, when the latitude is considered. As far north as Cook Inlet it compares very well with that of England and Scotland. The precipitation in Prince William Sound is extremely heavy, and in early April we found snow in Portage Bay from 6 to 7 feet deep on the level; while in Cook Inlet, on the other hand, which is sheltered from the moisture-laden winds of the Japan Current by the mountain mass of Kenai Peninsula, precipitation is very much lighter. Here no frost is to be feared from the 1st of June until the 1st of September, and the temperature gets quite high enough to mature the hardier vegetables. Passing up the Matanuska Valley through the Coast Range, however, the traveler notes a great change. The equable climate of the coast yields to a climate of great extremes just within the Coast Range. The summers are very short and uncomfortably hot, and the winters long and severe; the snowfall is not great, seldom reaching more than 18 inches. The summers from the 1st of May until about the 1st of July are relatively dry; then a rainy season sets in, usually lasting three or four weeks. Following this, before snowfall begins, is a period of bright, clear, cool autumn weather, which is the best time of the entire season for work, since the insect pests have then disappeared.

AGRICULTURE.

A few experiments have been conducted in Cook Inlet in the raising of the hardier grains and vegetables. Last year potatoes sufficient to partially supply the Sunrise City mining district were raised at Tyonek. Lettuce, turnips, and radishes of excellent quality were also grown, and rye has been reported to have been raised successfully in the past. Some hardy varieties of wheat were sown this fall, and there seems no reason why this important food plant should not mature here. The Russians have successfully raised cattle, the abundant meadows of natural grass furnishing pasture during the summer and hay for the winter months. In the interior the greater severity of the winter and the shorter growing season make it improbable that anything except the very hardiest vegetables can ever be raised.

INHABITANTS.

Five hundred to a thousand white men, usually prospectors and claim owners, generally winter about the head of Cook Inlet. This number is more than doubled during the summer; but this population is essentially transient, and the great majority of the prospectors never penetrate more than 30 or 40 miles from the coast.

The native inhabitants are assembled in colonies at Tyonek, Ladds Station, and Knik. They do not number, all told, more than a few hundred souls, and this number is constantly diminishing through pulmonary complaints. In character they are gentle, harmless, and surprisingly honest. Along the route which we followed to the interior very few Indians were seen, chiefly because our line of travel lay along the divides, while the permanent homes of the Indians are found along the great waterways, which are their lines of travel. Two hundred and seventy-five miles from Knik we met a small band of Upper Copper River Indians on a hunting trip along the head waters of the Delta River, and another band was encountered near the same point on the return trip. A Matanuska Indian village is situated on a small lake draining into Taxlina River near the head of the Matanuska, and smoke from the hunting lodges of members of this tribe was noticed at several points along the lower course of Bubb Creek.

REPORT ON PRINCE WILLIAM SOUND AND THE COPPER RIVER REGION.[1]

By F. C. SCHRADER.

ITINERARY.

The United States Army Copper River Alaskan Expedition No. 2, of 1898, to which the writer was attached, left Seattle on the steamship *Valencia* April 7 and landed at Port Valdez, Alaska, on April 19. At the beach the snow was 6½ feet deep, and our tents were pitched in deep pits dug in it. As the reindeer counted on for transportation had not been brought, our camp remained here until August 5, when, with a pack train of 23 horses, a hasty and somewhat hazardous trip of nearly two days was made across the Valdez glacier, over the Coast Mountains, 5,000 feet high, and into the Copper River drainage, our objective field of work. As the season was now already far advanced, it was apparent that a survey to the head of the Copper and the Mount Wrangell district would be impossible. The work of the writer was therefore carried down the Klutena to Copper Center on the Copper River, then down the Copper to the mouth of the Tasnuna, and thence westward, closing the circuit to Valdez by way of Tasnuna and Lowe rivers.

During most of the time spent in the interior, from late in August till the return to Valdez on October 19, one party of the expedition was in charge of the writer, who carried on the geologic work, while the topography was done principally by Mr. Emil Mahlo. Two other parties were in charge of Captain Abercrombie and of Lieutenant Lowe, respectively; of these the former proceeded to Mentasta Pass and the latter to Fortymile on the Yukon.

From Valdez to the Tonsina River the work was carried on by transit. By the wrecking of a raft in crossing the Tonsina the transit was lost, and the remainder of the circuit was completed by compass. From Valdez to Taral transportation was principally by pack train, although some supplies were sent down from Copper Center by boat; but at Taral all further progress with the pack train was cut off by Woods Canyon, whose walls slope up into high snow-peaked mountains on either side. From this point to the mouth of the Tasnuna, therefore, travel was by boat; and thence, packing on the backs of

[1] See maps Nos. 7 and 8, in accompanying envelope.

men, the journey up the Tasnuna was continued over a divide about 1,800 feet high, down Lowe River to Dutch Camp Basin, and from that basin by pack train into Valdez.

GEOGRAPHY.

Prince William Sound is a large bay lying between 60° and 61° north latitude and 146° and 149° west longitude. It is bounded on the north and northeast by the mainland, on the west by the Kenai Peninsula, and on the south by numerous islands. The many deep indentations of the coast line on the north, with the outlying islands, present natural harbor facilities of the highest class for even the largest ocean vessels.

Nearly north of the sound, but separated from it by a high, rugged range of coast mountains, is the Copper River Basin, whose drainage extends northward to the parallel 63° 30'; the river itself, upon breaking through the range, debouches over a large delta into the Gulf of Alaska, just east of Prince William Sound.

POPULATION.

Prince William Sound natives.—The natives about Prince William Sound, probably several hundred in all, are known as Aleuts. They have long been under missionary influence, mainly Russian. Their chief settlements or villages are Tatilak, Nuchek, Chenega, Eyak, and Allaghanik. They trade with the whites and are often employed by them, chiefly in hunting, fishing, and boating. They are not a very healthy people, consumptive tendencies among them being common.

Prince William Sound whites.—About a dozen white men have married into the native tribes and have become residents there, being engaged in trade or some other industry, such as blue fox raising.

At Orca and Eyak are large salmon canneries, owned by American companies and operated during the summer months only. The labor employed here is mostly Chinese, imported from San Francisco for each season only. Orca is also a United States post-office, with monthly mails.

Copper River natives.—The Copper River natives are distinct from the Aleut tribes on the coast and seem to be more closely allied to the North American Indian; their total number is probably less than 300. The country is apportioned off politically, each clan adhering closely to its own district in hunting and fishing. Until recently those best known to the whites were the Taral or Chittyna natives, whose chief, Nicolai, has been mentioned by Lieutenant Allen, Lieutenant Schwatka, and Dr. Hayes. Nicolai, however, has now lost his influence among his people, who with unanimous praise refer to Hanegatta as the most wealthy, powerful, and capable leader of their tribe. The Tezlinas and Gakonas, constituting the Upper Copper River natives, are commonly known as the Kolchanes; they are said to number about 200, the Tezlinas about 125, and the Gakonas some 60 or 80. The Tezlinas occupy the country from the Copper River westward along the Tezlina River and Lake to Knik River. The country from above Lake Klutena down the Copper to near Taral is occupied by the "Stick" natives, headed by the sturdy chief Stiphan.

The Copper River natives, on the whole, seem to be honest. Though poor, they are hospitable and obliging people, and on several occasions last summer they saved the lives and property of whites who had gone astray.

Prospectors and explorers.—Owing probably very largely to the liberal advertisement of passage to the Copper River country by transportation companies, many prospectors and adventurers bound for the Klondike or to indefinite destinations in Alaska were led, in the season of 1898, to try their fortunes in the Copper River country. Many hoped at the same time to proceed by way of the prospective all-American route into the gold districts of the Upper Yukon.

The influx began in February and continued until late in June, during which time it is estimated that more than 4,000 persons and their outfits landed at Valdez, the great gateway to the Copper. Of these, more than 3,000 are supposed to have entered the Copper River Basin over the summit of the Valdez glacier. In the meantime several hundred prospectors landed at Orca and attempted to ascend the Copper River from its mouth, but very few of them reached Taral and the Chittyna.

The exodus began early in May and continued until late in October, many returning over the glacier to Valdez afoot and many down the Copper by boat. Probably 300 remained in the country, mostly at Copper Center, during the winter of 1898–99, and a score or so at Valdez on the coast. Among those in the interior numerous cases of scurvy, some of which were serious, are reported to have occurred.

The letter mail taken from Valdez into the Copper River during the three months of August, September, and October numbered more than 4,200. Applications for the establishment of an official post-office at Valdez and at Copper Center are now on the files of the Postmaster-General.

CLIMATE.

Prince William Sound.—The climate at Prince William Sound is mild, with a high average percentage of cloudiness, very heavy precipitation, and great barometric range.

Spring, midsummer, and a part of the fall are rainy and foggy. The annual snowfall is from 7 to 10 feet. Fierce blasts are said to occur in winter.

During the summer of 1898 the weather at Valdez was as follows:

From April 24 to May 1: continuous heavy snowfall, with some thawing; little or no wind.
May: generally rainy, foggy, and mild.
June 1 to about July 10: fine weather, generally bright and sunny; middays warm but not hot; temperature generally comfortable to cool; little or no fog
July 10 to August 10: generally rainy and foggy.

Valdez summit.—The summit is almost constantly enveloped in storm and fog, with precipitation nearly always in the solid state.

Copper River district.—The change of climate experienced in a couple of hours' travel—7 or 8 miles—from the bleak, frigid, and stormy summit down into the Copper River Basin in August is remarkable. Here the slopes are clothed with timber, variegated flowers, grasses, and berries, while the clear bright skies rival the halcyon summer days of the Upper Yukon or the rainless districts of western United States.

According to the reports of prospectors the summer months are bright and warm, with midday often hot; night frost may occur at any time, but is very rare in June, July, and early August. The streams begin to freeze late in October, and snow to fall a few weeks later. The annual snowfall is from 2 to 4 feet. The winter seems to be much the same as on the Upper Yukon, though not quite so cold; but it is a storm-ridden country, swept by fierce blasts descending from the interior to the coast.

ANIMAL LIFE.

Fish.—In the lakelets in the Copper River country several species of handsome lake trout occur, but the fish most relied upon for subsistence by the natives is the salmon, notably the king salmon, which normally ascends the Copper and its tributaries in great numbers annually. Large quantities had already been dried by the prospectors on Lake Klutena early in August, and the fish were still running late in September between Taral and Copper Center.

Quadrupeds.—There is large game in the Copper Basin—several species of bear, caribou, and some moose. In the mountains toward the coast Rocky Mountain sheep were shot by prospectors, and wolf are also said to occur. Beaver are present on most of the tributaries and lakelets. Red and gray squirrel, though usually of small size, are abundant throughout the timber. No rabbits were seen by us, though they were long ago reported by Allen. Porcupine are common. A species of field mouse was seen, and a third-grown or dwarf frog.

Birds.—The eagle, black crow, hawk, goose, duck, ptarmigan, grouse, sea gull, sandpiper, snowbird, American robin, brown thrush, oriole, blackbird, woodpecker, and many other migratory species of birds were seen.

Insects.—During the months of May, June, and July the mosquito is a veritable pest. Sand flies and gnats also occur later in the season. Flies, grasshoppers, beetles, butterflies, moths, and several species of Neuroptera were seen on the mountain slopes at the foot of Lake Klutena late in August.

VEGETATION.

Prince William Sound.—About Prince William Sound the chief timber is spruce, sometimes called Sitka spruce, with some yellow cedar, cottonwood, willow, and alder. The poplar is usually confined to the flats in the mouths of the valleys and inlets, where some good grass also occurs. The timber line is about 2,000 feet, above which only moss and dwarf shrubbery grow. All the hardier garden vegetables were successfully grown in Valdez last summer.

Copper River district.—In the Copper River district the country is comparatively well, though not densely, timbered. Spruce is the dominant and most valuable tree and has a good, tall growth; hemlock, aspen, balm of Gilead, birch, poplar, alder, and willow are also present. The timber line scarcely reaches to 2,000 feet. Though the surface is normally clothed with a dense growth of moss, large areas of good grass also occur, the grasses representing half a dozen or more species, some of which resemble the silver-top, red-top, and blue-joint of the Western States. They are of a rank, succulent growth, and often 3 or more feet high, excellent for grazing and seemingly good for hay purposes. Wild flowers, many species of which are identical with those found in the States, occur in great abundance. In luxuriance of growth the wild roses along the Copper greatly surpass anything ever seen by the writer in the States. The ripened hips of the roses are much used by the natives as food, and in the absence of fruit diet the members of the party also partook of them with much relish. In many localities wild red currants occur in great abundance, also great quantities of the moss berry, or ground cranberry; and the black currant, gooseberry, blueberry, huckleberry, red salmon berry, red raspberry, cranberry, and a kind of Viburnum, or high-bush light-red cranberry, are also found.

From early June to the close of the season of 1898 all the ordinary garden vegetables were successfully grown at Copper Center by Mr. Jacob Sittel, a gardener from Portland, Oregon.

TOPOGRAPHY.

Prince William Sound has the topography of a submerged coast, its deep inlets, fiords, and bays denoting the lower reaches of former subaerial valleys, while the outlying islands represent the crests of mountainous ridges whose bases are now under water.

From below Orca northward the relief of the country changes from rather rounded, low, and somewhat dome-shaped hills to steep or almost abrupt-faced mountains 2,000 to 4,000 feet in height, which often terminate in sharp peaks. These steep slopes are especially characteristic of the inner portions of the bays and inlets which almost everywhere deeply indent the coast. Farther northward, on the peninsula of the Chugatch Mountains, and continuing northwestward and northward beyond Port Valdez into the Copper River Basin, and from Valdez eastward across the Copper seemingly as far as the Mount St. Elias district, the topography is of a much rougher and more exclusively mountainous and jagged character. The general land mass, which here rises from 4,000 to 5,000 feet above sea level and ascends gently northward like a slightly tilted plateau, presents a surface considerably dissected and freely studded by sharp, jagged peaks, turrets, and broken or discontinuous sawtooth ridges, often interspersed with névé and local glaciers of moderate size. This type of topography is largely due to the character and attitude of the rocks, which almost everywhere are steeply upturned. The amphitheaters or cirques, which are common at the base of many peaks and ridges, constitute a modification of the otherwise normal topography, brought about through the agency of ice or local glaciers at points where the topography and atmospheric conditions have favored the accumulation of precipitation in the solid form. Where cut through by the Copper River this coastal range of mountains extends northward to Taral and the Chittyna River, about 100 miles distant from the coast. Just above these points the mountains soon recede westward, inclosing on their north and northeast the rather extensive moss- and timber-covered plateau-like basin of the upper part of the Copper.

This coastal range, which thus forms the broad barrier between the coast and the basin proper of the Copper River, and through which, in a deep, mountainous, canyon-like valley, the Copper has cut its way to the coast, is probably post-Pliocene in age and may be considered a westward continuation of the St. Elias Range.

Between Prince William Sound and the Copper River Basin these mountains differ from most other mountain ranges in the fact that they terminate rather abruptly along the coast on the south and along the edge of the Copper River Basin on the north. Also on the northwest they terminate rather abruptly in an extensive tundra plateau which forms the northwest rim of the Copper Basin and constitutes the poorly defined watershed between this drainage and that of the Sushitna on the west. According to Mr. Mendenhall, this divide has an average elevation of about 2,800 or 2,900 feet; it extends from the north base of the mountains in the vicinity of Lake Taslina northeastward to the Alaskan Mountains.

About 25 miles east of the Copper River, and inclosed by its big bend, the snow-covered Mount Wrangell group of mountains rises to a maximum height of more than 17,000 feet. These mountains are the terminus of a northwestward spur or branch of the St. Elias Range, being separated from the westward or main range by the Chittyna River, the great eastern tributary of the Copper. Although little explored, they have for some time been regarded as volcanic. Mount Drum has much the form of a large volcanic cone; Mount Tillman is gently rounded, with its longer axis extending northwest and southeast; and Mount Blackburn, the most southeasterly of the group, rises to a height of 12,500 feet, its longer axis coinciding in direction with that of Tillman.

GEOLOGY.

Orca series.—Beginning below Orca in Prince William Sound and extending northward and northwestward, the rocks are a sedimentary series, consisting of thick-bedded brown and gray sandstones and arkoses interlarded with usually thin layers of shale or slate and occasionally some conglomerate. The general strike is a little north of east, or about E.-W.; the dip is steeply N. The rocks are freely jointed, often intensely folded and minutely faulted, and are traversed by three or more sets of cleavages. These cleavage planes are often followed by quartz and calcite veinlets.

Valdez series.—Farther to the west and northwest, in the vicinity of Fidalgo Bay and Copper Mountain, the rocks become more highly metamorphosed and consist of bluish-gray and dark quartzites, or arkoses, and quartz-schists, interbedded with generally thin beds of dark-blue or black slate, shale, mica-schist (sometimes slightly graphitic), nodular mica-schist, and occasionally some stretched conglomerate.

The strike and dip of these rocks, well shown in Port Valdez, are the same as in the Orca rocks, and the series extends northward over the range down into the Copper River Basin, and eastward across the Copper from below the Tasnuna up to near the foot of Woods Canyon below Taral. The rocks show much the same faulting, folding, and cleavage as the Orca rocks. They are at times cut by granitic diorite or aplite dikes.

Age of the Valdez and Orca series.—Fragmentary plant remains collected from both the Orca and the Valdez rocks are pronounced by Mr. F. H. Knowlton, of the United States Geological Survey, as probably Sequoia and Taxodium, referring the rocks to Upper Cretaceous or Lower Tertiary in age.

Copper Mountain greenstone or amphibolite-schist.—Exposed on the north shore of Prince William Sound, along the zone where the Orca rocks give way to the Valdez series, and trending nearly east and west, runs a somewhat mountainous backbone or ridge of green amphibolite-schist. It is a totally different rock from either the Orca or the Valdez series, but seems to underlie and greatly exceed them in age. On the sound it is best exposed to the east of Tatitlak, where it constitutes almost the entire mass of Copper Mountain, which rises steeply 5,000 feet above the sea; thence it extends eastward under Fidalgo Bay and across country toward the Copper River. In the Copper River Basin it forms the mountains along the south side of the Tonsina Valley, and from these mountains it continues southward to Woods Canyon, and thence eastward for some distance. It probably also forms the frontal ranges which come down toward the Copper from the Mount Wrangell group, on the southwest.

Klutena series.—The Valdez rocks, roughly speaking, extend northward to near the bend of Lake Klutena, where they give way to mica and quartz schists, sometimes jaspery, and marble. These rocks may for convenience be called the Klutena series; they resemble in some respects the rocks of the Fortymile series in the Yukon district.

Igneous rocks.—Above Orca, about Sheep Bay and Gravina Point, the beach is sometimes for miles lined with granitic diorite bowlders, whose large size and numbers would seem to favor the occurrence of the parent bed rock near by. Pebbles showing the contact of diabase with the Orca sedimentaries occur along the beach about Gravina Point and northward, and on the north shore of Blighs Island a typical medium-grained iron-gray diabase meets the darker slate; this is probably only a large dike. A somewhat similar rock occurs at the head of the Klutena River. Gabbro is found about 8 miles below Lake Klutena, on the northwest side of the Klutena River, in a hill rising about 1,100 feet above the river.

The rocks of the Mount Wrangell group have long been supposed to be volcanic, but as they have never been visited by any scientist nothing definite is known of them. Specimens received from Messrs. Cantwell and Mason, who in the summer of 1898 had penetrated to and collected from the north "crater" of Mount Drum, were pronounced by the writer, from hand-specimen examination, to be a red rhyolite and probably a gray andesite. The prospectors reported that the entire mass of Drum, as far as seen, is made up principally of this red rhyolite, and that it extends over many thousand square miles northward around and beyond Mount Sanford.

Copper River silts.—These beds form the plateau terrane of the Copper River Basin. They are composed for the most part of fine-grained, light buff-colored, unconsolidated silts, with local deposits of sand and gravel. The stratification is horizontal, and this, with the fineness of the material and the areal extent of the beds over the basin, probably more than 2,000 square miles, leads to the view that they were most probably deposited in some large lake or branch of the sea. The beds are exposed in the form of bluffs and terraces along the Copper River above Taral, and on the tributaries of that section of the river, often rising steeply from the river to a height of 400 or 500 feet; and they probably exceed 1,000 feet in maximum thickness. Geologically the beds seem to be very young. They nowhere show tendency to consolidation, nor do they seem to carry any fossils other than recent shells, occasionally found near the tops of the beds, of organisms such as now live along some of the streams in that district.

MINERAL RESOURCES.

COPPER.

About Prince William Sound it is common to find iron and copper sulphides disseminated almost anywhere throughout the country rock; but on some of the larger islands of the sound, and at several localities on the shore of the mainland, occur mineralized zones of considerable extent and of very promising economic value. The worth of the ores rests chiefly in their copper value, but in some of them gold and silver have also been assayed in good paying quantities.

Copper Mountain mine.—At Copper Mountain near Tatiklak, in Landlock Bay, where one of these deposits is being mined by the Alaska Commercial Company, the ore as observed by Mr. J. E. Spurr occupies a shear zone in the green amphibolite-schist, and consists principally of copper pyrites and bornite. It is best exposed about 300 feet above sea level.

On the northwest base of the mountain, facing the head of Copper Mountain Bay, a somewhat similar deposit occurs, known as the Ripstein ledge.

Gladhaugh Bay mine.—Just above Tatiklak, in the head of Gladhaugh Bay, a vein or deposit consisting mostly of iron and copper pyrites and about 600 feet in width is being worked by a Vancouver company. The contact of an igneous rock (diabase) with the country rock here seems to have something to do with the ore deposit.

Latouche and Knights islands.—Other localities which are receiving considerable attention and are being developed are Knights and Latouche islands. On the latter, which lies in the southern part of the sound, the deposit seems to be a phenomenally large one. The ore is mostly bornite and copper pyrites, and is of good grade, frequently running as high as 25 per cent copper to the ton, with from $1 to $3 in gold and silver.

Up in the Copper River country native copper in small amount was long ago found in possession of the natives. Its source is supposed to be the Chittyna and Upper White River districts. Prospectors who ascended the Chittyna in the summer of 1898 report the prospects of copper good, and display nuggets of the native metal 3 inches in diameter. North of the Chittyna the Stick natives report the best source of copper to be up the tributaries coming down from the southwest base of the Mount Wrangell group; while the Taral natives, so far as can be learned, are probably familiar with a considerable deposit of the metal or its ore up the Chittystone, or southeast fork of the Chittyna, each tribe being best acquainted with that in its own district.

GOLD-BEARING QUARTZ.

The quartz found in the country rock usually occurs in discontinuous stringers or veinlets and not in large quantities. Assays of samples collected at several points show it to carry gold, which is probably the source of the placer or fine gold found disseminated in the gravels throughout the country. So far as the observations of the writer extend, the country can hardly be considered promising for gold-quartz mining. One assay, however, collected by the writer from Wilson Point in Prince William Sound, yielded 1.25 ounces of gold, and 3 ounces of silver, or a total money value of about $27 to the ton. The vein (which was discovered by the writer) is about 3 feet in thickness and is an aggregate stringer vein, being made up of a great many parallel quartz stringers or veinlets trending with the bedding of the rock. It is probably a shear-zone deposit. Its dip is nearly vertical. No idea of its linear extent was formed, as it soon passed beneath the deep covering of moss and snow; it seems, however, to warrant further investigation and probably development.

PLACERS.

About the most of Prince William Sound and in the Copper River country, gold placer digging is yet in its early stages. The considerable prospecting, however, which has been done seems to indicate that the country as a whole is not very promising in this line, although fine or flour gold occurs almost everywhere, both in the gravels on the coast and in the Copper River district.

Several years ago gravels at the mouth of Mineral Creek, which flows into Port Valdez, are reported to have yielded fair pay to several pioneers who worked them. Some work was also done on the south side of the sound, in Solomons Basin, with similar results, and recently in Canyon Creek Bay some coarse gold has been sluiced. Claims are staked off at various locations, some in the terminal moraine gravels at the foot of the Valdez glacier. Some coarse gold has also been panned from the gravels in Dutch Camp Basin.

In the Copper River country the thick deposit of gravels and lake beds, which during most of the summer carry considerable water, is a great impediment to effectual prospecting. According to seemingly reliable prospectors, good coarse gold was found last summer on a branch of the Slana River near the head waters of the Copper, and on Quartz Creek, one of the upper tributaries of the Tonsina, where many claims are reported staked and some men are wintering. Mr. Charles Brown, United States Quatermaster at Valdez, has lately reported that men are working on Manker Creek and Mahlo River, both tributaries to the Klutena, and on some of the head waters of the Teikell.

COAL.

So far as seen by the writer the formations met with seem to be barren of coal. It may be mentioned, however, that on the Upper Gakona River some prospectors report the occurrence of coal in workable quantities.

ROUTES AND TRAILS.

The only route used for getting into the Copper River country from Valdez during the season of 1898 was the Valdez glacier route. Starting from Valdez, the trail leads 4 miles northeast, with a very gentle rise over the delta gravels, to the foot of the Valdez glacier, thence about north for 18 miles up the glacier to the summit, which is 4,800 feet high. The glacier is broken or transversely marked by four or five successive long benches or terraces, from one to the other of which the rise of 100 feet or more is usually sharp and sometimes difficult, the topography of the ice being very rugged, with crevasses, ridges, and turrets. With the exception of these benches the ascent from the foot of the glacier to near the summit is gradual; but just before reaching the top there is a steep rise of a thousand feet at an angle of 15° to 20°. The pass is guarded by a couple of prominent peaks, one on either side and standing about a mile apart. From the summit the trail descends rapidly, but nowhere abruptly, for a distance of 6 miles through a canyon-like valley to the foot of the Klutena glacier, which is the source of the Klutena River.

From the foot of the Valdez glacier to the foot of the Klutena glacier, a distance of 25 miles, there is no vegetation, timber, or brush, but only a waste of barren rock walls, peaks, and snow and ice, so that fuel for camping while on the glacier must be brought from either end. From the foot of the Klutena glacier the trail continues down the north side of the river and lake to Copper Center, where the elevation is about 1,050 feet.

From Copper Center to the Tanana, Yukon, and Fortymile rivers, the best and shortest route is the Millard trail by way of Mentasta Pass. This trail, crossing the Copper, bears northeastward somewhat near the base of Mounts Drum and Sanford, over the high ground of the big bend of the Copper, and is said to be a good, cut horse trail from Copper Center to near the Copper River below the mouth of the Slana. From Copper Center another route leads along the northwest side of the Copper River to the mouth of the Slana; this trail, however, is much longer than and not so good as the Millard trail.

From the northwest bend of Lake Klutena at Cranberry Marsh a trail branches off up Salmon Creek Valley and leads by way of Lake Lily northward to the Tazlina River, thence down that river to the Copper. This route seems to have been started chiefly by prospectors before the snow disappeared in the spring of 1898, after which the marshiness of the country over which it ran led to its disuse. That part of it down the Tazlina, however, is an Indian trail, and is said to be pretty fair and to continue westward down the Matanuska and Knik rivers to Cook Inlet. Long ago it was in use by the Russians in traveling from Cook Inlet to Copper River.

Previous maps have reported a good trail from Taral northward on both sides of the Copper. This is a mistake, for although portions of a trail are here and there met with, they are liable at any time to run out, usually extending but a short distance from the native villages. The Survey party, in coming down the Copper to Taral, found it necessary to cut trail most of the way. From Taral southward, on the east side of the Copper River, there is a portage trail of about 4 miles, for foot only, to the lower end of Woods Canyon, from which point southward through the mountains there is no trail save that recently cut by prospectors at difficult points for towing up boats. An Indian trail is said to ascend the Chittyna River from Taral to above the forks, but is not suitable for pack animals.

A proposed route from Valdez into the Copper River country starts up Lowe River Valley, which it would leave at Dutch Camp Basin, and, bearing off to the north, would cross the head waters of the Tonsina and, descending Manker Creek Valley, strike the Klutena River and trail just below the lake. It runs over some unexplored country, but seems to be by far the most suitable of all for railroad and pack-train purposes. At the head of the Tonsina a branch trail strikes off to Sawmill camp just below Twelvemile camp. Some engineering will be required through Keystone Canyon on Lowe River to make the trail practicable for all-summer travel.

Another feasible route would be from Valdez up Lowe River, across the divide (which is only 1,800 feet high), and down the Tasnuna River to the Copper, whence the transportation up the Copper would be by boat, preferably a light-draft steamer of special power.

Table of approximate distances from Valdez by Glacier trail to Copper Center and thence by Millard trail to Mentasta Pass.

Place.	Miles.	Elevation in feet.
Valdez	0	0
Foot of Valdez glacier	4	210
Top of third bench	8	830
Twelvemile camp, at foot of fourth bench	16	2,750
Foot of summit	22	3,800
Summit	23	4,800
Foot of Klutena glacier	29	2,020
Onemile camp	30	1,960
Twelvemile camp	33	1,930
Sawmill camp	35	1,740
Twentyfourmile camp, at head of Lake Klutena	46	1,673
Cranberry Marsh	64	1,673
Foot of Lake Klutena	79	1,670
Amee Landing	85	1,370
Coxe Landing	90	1,320
Cook Bend	95	1,240
Bowlder Spring, on bluff	97	1,590
Copper Center, at mouth of Klutena	112	1,050
Mentasta Pass (by Millard trail)	205	2,300

REPORT OF THE WHITE RIVER-TANANA EXPEDITION.[1]

By W. J. PETERS and ALFRED H. BROOKS.

NARRATIVE.

The party on whose work the following report is based was constituted as follows: W. J. Peters, topographer in charge; Alfred H. Brooks, geologist; Charles Ray, H. B. Baker, A. R. Airs, and L. D. Gardiner, camp hands. We desire to express our indebtedness to these four men for services faithfully rendered, under what were frequently very trying conditions.

Our party crossed the White Pass, on the snow, about the middle of April, and made its way on the ice to the head of Marsh Lake. Here we were delayed for several weeks on account of the spring thaw; finally, the ice having broken, we started down the lake in our canoes on the 28th of May. During the first few days we were much hampered by ice floes, which forced us to make several portages and rendered canoe navigation rather perilous. After passing Lake Lebarge we saw no more of the ice, and traveled rapidly down the river. At Fort Selkirk we attempted to obtain information from the Indians in regard to the region we were to explore, but in this we met with a very moderate degree of success and the results were not encouraging. We were assured that it would be impossible to ascend the White River in boats, and the portage to the Tanana was estimated as from 20 to 100 miles in length. According to these stories, if we escaped the perils of navigating the White and Tanana rivers we ran still greater dangers from the Tanana Indians, who were said to guard their country jealously from the intrusion of white men.

On June 5 we reached the mouth of White River, where Mr. Barnard and party, with whom we had traveled thus far, left us to continue their journey to the Fortymile region. On June 8 our party of six made a start up the White River, with provisions for three months and equipment divided among three canoes. The ascent of the river was accomplished under great difficulties; by tracking (cordelling), poling, and much of the time dragging the canoes, we reached the mouth of Snag River by July 10. Through the hardest kind of work, which included almost continuous wading and frequent duckings in the glacial waters of the White River, we had in a month made about 85 miles. We were hampered not only by the swift current but also by the numerous quicksands, as well as the many snags found in the

---

[1] See map No. 9, in accompanying envelope.

river, on which our canoes were frequently injured so as to require repairs. This month was, however, not entirely spent on the river, for we made several trips inland to extend our geologic and topographic mapping.

After continuing up Snag River some 65 miles we found a portage to Tanana waters which was but a few miles in length; here, in a broad lowland, Mirror Creek, a tributary of the Tanana, has its source within a few miles of Snag River. The portage was accomplished in a few days, and then, to the great delight of all the party, we started down a smoothly flowing, clear-water stream, our progress contrasting strongly with that of the previous six weeks. Mirror Creek proved to be about 60 miles in length, and enters the Tanana near its great westerly bend, probably 40 or 50 miles from the source of the latter stream. The month of August was spent in traversing and making a hasty survey of some 500 miles of the Tanana River. At the point near the Mentasta Pass and Fortymile trail we met some prospectors and Indians, the first human beings we had seen in two months. We reached Weare, at the mouth of the Tanana, on the 1st of September, as had been planned, with our provisions entirely exhausted. From Weare we went down the Yukon by river steamer, and from St. Michael returned to Seattle.

PREVIOUS EXPLORATIONS.

The Upper White was explored in 1891 by Lieutenant Schwatka and Dr. Hayes, who crossed by overland trail from Fort Selkirk and reached the river some 150 miles above its mouth. They continued their journey to the source of the White, and crossed to the Copper River by way of the Scolai Pass.[1] A portion of the Tanana was explored in 1885 by Lieutenant Allen, who, with a small party, crossed from the Copper River by the Suslota Pass and continued down the Tanana to its mouth.[2] Different parts of these river basins have also been visited by those indefatigable explorers, the Alaskan prospectors; but unfortunately the information collected by them is seldom exact and is as a rule not easily available.

GEOGRAPHY.

The White and Tanana drainage systems comprise the larger part of the drainage basin of the Yukon which lies to the south of that great river. A description of the general geographic features of these two basins will be found in the sketch of the geography of the Yukon district (p. 85) and will not be repeated here. The White and Tanana rivers and their tributaries lie for the most part in the

---

[1] A trip to the Yukon Basin, by C. Willard Hayes: Nat. Geog. Mag., Vol. IV, 1892, pp. 117-162.
[2] An Exploration of the Copper, Tanana, and Koyukuk Rivers in the Territory of Alaska, by Lieut. Henry T. Allen, U. S. A.

dissected upland which has been called the Yukon Plateau. Several mountain groups which mark the southern limits of these basins rise abruptly from this upland, and their rugged slopes and jagged crests contrast strongly with the flat-topped remnants of the old plateau. These snow-clad mountains lying along the southern margin can be differentiated into three groups. The most easterly of these is the great St. Elias Range, of which Dr. Hayes says:[1]

> Like the southern coast range, it is a broad, elevated belt, with numerous peaks and short ridges, probably the highest being along its southern border, culminating in Mount St. Elias. Westward from this peak the range is separated into two divergent ranges by the valley of the Chittenah River. The one continued to the northwest contains high volcanic peaks of the Wrangell group.

The Nutzotin Mountains, the second of these groups, lie to the south of the Upper Tanana Valley, and in these the Tanana probably heads. This range has a NW.-SE. trend and an elevation of 8,000 to 10,000 feet; it lies to the north of the Upper White River Valley, and hence to the north of the St. Elias Range, and in its northwesterly extension divides the Copper and the Tanana waters. The range is entirely unexplored, and its exact topographic relations are not known. To the northwest it decreases in altitude, the peaks here ranging from 6,000 to 7,000 feet in height, while the Mentasta and Suslota passes, which are decided breaks in the range, are probably not over 4,000 feet high. West of Mentasta Pass the divide increases in elevation until it finally merges into the Alaskan Range.

The Alaskan Range extends in a southwesterly direction from the Middle Tanana, and is broken by several broad gaps, such as the valleys of the Delta and Cantwell rivers. It is possible that further explorations will show that the Nutzotin Mountains represent an eastern extension of the same uplift.

To the west of the Alaskan Range we have little information in regard to the limits of the Tanana Basin. The divide between the Tanana and Kuskokwim waters was far distant from our route of travel and we were unable to determine its character. It is probably a range of mountains of no great elevation, which decreases in height and gradually bends to the southward as it approaches the Yukon.

In its lower course the White River cuts through a mountain mass whose highest summits mark the level of the old plateau, in the western extension of which are the sources of several tributaries of the White, Tanana, Sixtymile, and Fortymile rivers. A depression separates this upland from the Ketchumstock Hills, which continue the divide between the Yukon and the Tanana waters; this minor range is probably higher than the old upland, and is itself separated from the Tanana Hills by the gap of the Chena River.

---

[1] Op. cit., p. 129.

The White River rises in the north lobe of the Russell glacier, and flows east through a broad valley for 40 miles parallel with the St. Elias Range, receiving numerous tributaries from the mountains to the south. Below this flat the valley gradually narrows and assumes a canyon-like character, and then in a distance of 20 miles debouches on a broad lowland. This lowland has a length of about 75 miles and an extreme width of 50 miles; it embraces not only the White River and some confluent streams, but is extended through to the Tanana in broad, flat valleys. It is interrupted here and there by knobs, hills, and mountain masses, which rise abruptly from the wooded plain. Below this lowland the White has a comparatively narrow valley all the way to its mouth.

Where we first reached the Tanana, at the mouth of Mirror Creek, it flows in a broad lowland which might be considered an extension of the valley of the White. The Tanana enters this plain through a narrow gap, above which it has not yet been explored. The river valley here has a quadrangular outline, as will be seen by referring to the accompanying map (No. 9). A study of the map will also show that the Tanana Valley is in fact characterized by a series of these valley lowlands having quadrilateral outlines and bounded by steep escarpments. These broad lowlands are connected by narrow stretches of valley. Below the mouth of the Silokh River the southern side of the valley recedes rapidly, and from this point to the junction with the Yukon it is at least 30 miles wide. Along this lower portion of the river the southern side of the valley is not mapped, but the north slope continues to give suggestions of this quadrangular character in a series of reentrant angles which the river closely follows. Throughout its course the Tanana hugs very closely the north side of the valley. The confluent streams from the north all have sluggish currents and usually deep channels, while those entering from the south are shallow and swift, often being veritable torrents.

GEOLOGY.

Nasina series.—From the mouth of the White River to Ladue Creek are exposed quartz-schists and quartz-mica-schists associated with white crystalline limestones, which have been grouped together under the name of the Nasina series. In the schists are found numerous basic igneous rocks which have been more or less sheared, and some larger masses of intrusive granite which are entirely massive. These rocks of the Nasina series have been somewhat deformed, since they occur as a series of open folds. This series is probably the equivalent of the Birch Creek schists and the Fortymile series; but as it was impossible to differentiate them into the two horizons, it was thought best to give them a local name until their identity with the rocks described by Spurr could be definitely established.

Basal gneissoid series.—Between Ladue Creek and the White River Flats the river cuts a series composed of mica-schists and gneisses, with numerous intrusives, both sheared and massive. The intrusives are both of a granitic and of a dioritic character. While the contact between this and the Nasina series was not seen, it seems probable, from the fact that the gneisses have suffered much metamorphism, that they are an older series. The gneisses are found again on the Tanana, extending from Mount Chusana to about the mouth of the Delta River. Along the Tanana this series contains large masses of granite, which is often porphyritic and in places has been altered to an augen-gneiss.

Tanana schists.—These schists are essentially quartz-mica rocks, in places true phyllites (mica-slates), and frequently graphitic. Impure limestones are sometimes found interbedded with these phyllites. These schists have been closely folded, and since the folding granite masses have been intruded. Their relation to the gneissoid series was not definitely determined, but they are believed to be younger and are probably the equivalent of some member of the Nasina series. They are typically exposed along the Tanana between the mouth of the Chena and Nilkoka rivers, and they also form the Bean Ridge north of Baker Creek. On the Upper Tanana, near the mouth of Scotty and Gardiner creeks, are found some phyllites and impure limestones which have been tentatively classed with the Tanana schists. The north sides of the valleys of Mirror and Snag rivers are made up of greenstones and greenstone-schists. These are altered basic igneous rocks which are believed to have been intruded in the Tanana schists.

Wellesley formation.—This is a heavy bed of massive conglomerate over a thousand feet thick, interlarded with beds of clay slates, frequently carbonaceous. It is of Devonian or Carboniferous age. The bowlders of the conglomerate are largely derived from the greenstones above described, but some are of massive quartzite. A few granite dikes were found cutting the associated slates. This formation is folded and faulted, and the slates are locally altered to phyllite. Wellesley Mountain is made up of this formation, and it also occurs in extensive exposures in the valley of Mirror Creek.

Nilkoka formation.—The rocks of this formation are greenish and reddish clay slates associated with some fine conglomerates and sandstones. They are closely folded, but unaltered, and are probably of Paleozoic age or younger. This formation occupies a belt between the Nilkoka River and Baker Creek.

Younger sedimentary rocks.—A few miles below the mouth of the Tok River, on the Tanana, were found a few exposures of a soft yellow sandstone which was very gently folded. It contained a few fragmentary plant remains, not sufficient to determine its horizon, but from its general character it seems probable that it is of Cenozoic age. A few basic dikes were found in it.

Igneous rocks.—The igneous rocks occurring as intrusions in the various formations have already been referred to. Besides these, small areas of andesitic and rhyolitic lavas were found at several localities.

Summary of the bed-rock geology.—The gneisses are believed to be the oldest rocks of the region. They are flanked on the north at the Lower White River by the Nasina series, and on the south by the Tanana schists and associated greenstones. In the Mirror Creek Valley the Tanana schists are unconformably overlain by the Wellesley formation. On the Lower Tanana the Tanana schists are found again north of the gneisses, and continue to be the country rock to the mouth of the river, except between the Nilkoka River and Baker Creek, a stretch which is occupied by the younger Nilkoka formation. The Nilkoka rocks seem to occupy a basin flanked on the other side by the older rocks.

From the White River west to near the Chena River the general strike is NW.-SE., while at the first exposures seen beyond the valley of the Chena the strike has swung around at right angles to its former direction and runs NE.-SW. This remarkable change in direction has already been noted in the general descriptions of the geology of the Yukon district. On the White and on the upper half of the Tanana a line of deformation at right angles to the dominant strike was noted.

Glacial phenomena.—The northern limit of general glaciation, as noted by Hayes, crosses the White near the mouth of the Donjek River. The valley of the White River proper has, however, been glaciated nearly to the mouth of the Klotassin. From our route of travel a number of glaciers were seen in the high mountains to the north, but there was no opportunity to visit them. Several valleys of the southern tributaries of the Tanana which have their sources in the snow-clad mountains have in recent times been occupied by glaciers. In the case of the Delta River the glacier must have blocked the entire valley, for the terminal moraine lies in part against the north wall of the valley.

Silts and gravels.—The White River Valley above the lower gorge contains numerous terraces and benches of silts and gravels, some of which are several hundred feet above the present river level. On the lower half of the Tanana similar terraces are found. Lack of space will not permit a detailed description and consideration of these phenomena. Fossil evidence goes to show that these deposits are in part fresh-water, lake and river beds; some may be marine deposits.

Volcanic ash.—Dawson and Hayes have described the white volcanic ash which is distributed over a large area about the head of the White River and along the lower courses of the Pelly and Lewes. We observed this ash on Snag River and traced it westward on the Tanana nearly to the mouth of the Tok. Throughout this region it is usually covered by a few inches of soil.

MINERAL RESOURCES.

GOLD.

So far as our information goes, no gold deposits were being mined in either the White or the Tanana basin last summer. About a year ago there was a stampede to the Lower White to stake quartz claims. There is also a story current that a prospector took out several thousand dollars on the Delta River about two years ago, but this has never been verified. The results of our own investigations, limited as they were to one line of travel, with seldom any opportunity to wash anything but the river bars, are not conclusive as to the presence or absence of workable gold deposits.

The Lower White River has been more or less visited by prospectors, but the Tanana may be considered almost a virgin field. Though in the aggregate many prospectors have made hurried trips through this valley, little or no thorough work has been done. These parties have usually reached the Tanana when their provisions were nearly exhausted and they were forced to build rafts and hurriedly push for the mouth of the river, doing but little prospecting along the river bars. Late last summer several parties reached the Tanana prepared to spend the winter, and it is only by such means that the work of prospecting in this inaccessible region can be properly done.

On the White River the Nasina series carries considerable mineralized quartz, and the smaller tributaries usually show colors in the gravels. From the fact that some gold has been found on the Selwyn River to the east, and that the rocks are probably the same as those that are gold bearing in the Fortymile and Sixtymile districts, it would seem as if there ought to be good chances for gold in this part of the White River Basin also. On the Tanana below the mouth of Mirror Creek colors are usually to be found in the river bars where these consist of sand and gravel. In the Tanana region quartz veins containing traces of gold were found in every formation that has been described. The gneisses contain quartz veins which in some cases give a trace of gold, and in one instance gold was found in a shear zone in the granite. The Tanana schists, both on the upper and on the lower river, are cut by quartz veins and by veins of quartz and calcite which contain some gold. A few quartz veins were observed in the slate of the Wellesley formation, and one of these which was analyzed carried a little gold. Some quartz veins in the Nilkoka formation were also found to contain traces of gold. In all the assays made of the gold-bearing quartz some silver was found with the gold, but in no case was the amount of gold and silver found in the veins of sufficient quantity to be of any commercial value.

All the southern tributaries of the Tanana between Robertson and Silokh rivers gave good colors. The streams entering the Tanana from the north have currents too sluggish to carry anything but flour gold. We would call attention to the fact that the gravel and sands of the river terraces here, as elsewhere in Alaska, frequently contain small amounts of gold, which, like the deposits in which it occurs, may be of more or less remote derivation. Such gold may find its way into the present river bars, and the finding of colors should therefore not be considered evidence of the presence of gold in the rocks of the vicinity.

COPPER.

There have long been traditions of copper deposits on the White and Tanana rivers as well as on the Copper. In 1891 Dr. Hayes was conducted by the Indians to the deposits on the White River from which they obtained their copper. This deposit, on Kletsan Creek near the head of the White River, proved to be a placer containing nuggets of native copper, the largest of which weighed several ounces.[1] Dr. Hayes was also shown some azurite which the Indians told him came from the White River region. There are fairly well authenticated stories of the finding of copper ores on the Upper Tanana. In our trip last summer we were unable to verify these stories by personal observation.

COAL.

Coal is said to exist in considerable quantities on some of the tributaries of the Tanana. Not having had time to explore any of the side streams, we are unable to substantiate these statements.

TIMBER.

What has been said elsewhere of the timber of the Yukon district applies equally to the Tanana and White rivers. According to the standard of the interior of Alaska, much good timber is to be found on both these rivers. The timber line is at an altitude of about 3,000 feet, and the chief varieties are cottonwood, spruce, white birch, alder, and willow. Forest fires are annually destroying much timber in the region.

GAME.

Moose, caribou, and several varieties of bear are common in many parts of the basins, while the mountain goat and the bighorn are found

---
[1] A trip to the Yukon Basin, by C. Willard Hayes; Nat. Geog. Mag., Vol. IV, 1892, pp. 144-145.

in the higher mountains. One of the chief sources of food supply of the natives are the salmon, which ascend the White probably as far as the Klotassin, and the Tanana to about the foot of Bates Rapids.

CLIMATE.

The climate, like that of most of the Yukon Basin, is semi-arid, with short hot summers and long cold winters. The accompanying table gives a summary of our meteorological observations.

Temperature observations on the White and Tanana rivers in 1898.

Month.	Minimum.	Maximum.	Rainy days.
June	42°	70°	3
July	42°	75°	10
August	41°	63°	8

AGRICULTURE.

The agricultural possibilities of the Yukon district have been treated elsewhere in this report; and what has been said there applies equally well to the Tanana region. The Tanana Valley has a rather more luxuriant vegetation than the White River Valley. Some of the hardier grains, potatoes, and vegetables could probably be grown there. The native grasses of the Tanana Flats are said to furnish excellent pasturage by those who have used pack horses in the region.

ROUTES AND MEANS OF TRANSPORTATION.

In the past, traveling in this region has been limited chiefly to the large waterways, on which boats and canoes were used in summer and sleds in winter. The development of the district will be rapidly advanced by the introduction of steamboat navigation on the Tanana and the use of pack animals throughout the entire region. Grass for stock will be found from about the 1st of June to the middle of September.

White River.—Navigation of the White River may be said to be almost entirely impracticable. It is possible, however, that the mouth of Ladue Creek might be reached in a shallow-draft boat with a powerful engine. The experience of our party last summer shows that the small boats or canoes can reach the mouth of Snag River, but it is doubtful whether this is an economical method of arriving at that point. Sledding up the White River on the ice has been done and is entirely feasible. This stream, on account of its swift current, is said to remain open a month later in the fall and to break a month earlier in the spring than the Yukon near the mouth of the White River.

Trails to White River.—The head of the White River could probably be reached by pack train from Lynn Canal. The Chilkat Indians are said to have had a route across the head of the White to the Tanana, which was used by them for trading with the Indians of the interior. It is reported that a party of miners crossed from Yakutat Bay to the White last summer. Last season Mr. J. B. Tyrrell traversed the region from Chilkat Inlet to the mouth of the Nissling. His report has not been published, but he tells us that the route is not a difficult one. The route from the Copper River over the Scolai Pass is not likely to recommend itself, because of the difficulty of ascending the Chittyna River. The Schwatka and Hayes route from Fort Selkirk to the White is entirely feasible for pack animals, but is not so favorable as the routes farther south. The Lower White can be reached from Sixtymile River by crossing the divide and coming down Ladue Creek.

Tanana River.—There are no serious difficulties in navigating the Tanana River up to the point where it broadens out above the mouth of the Cantwell, a distance of about 170 miles. From this point to where the Fortymile-Suslota trail crosses, the river can be ascended only by a steamer especially adapted for the purpose. Such a steamer must be capable of making progress against an 8-mile current and should have facilities for warping where it is necessary. In this portion of the river are usually many channels, and by carefully picking the route much of the swifter water can be avoided. A slough some 30 miles in length which is suitable for steamboat navigation is said to extend from below the mouth of the Chena River to the Salchacket, close to the north bank of the Tanana. From the Fortymile trail to Gardiner Creek the current of the Tanana is very moderate, and a flat-bottomed steam launch drawing not over 18 inches of water could easily navigate this part of the river.

Of the tributaries of the Tanana, the Goodpaster, Volkmar, Salchacket, Chena, and Toclat rivers could probably be ascended for some distance by small steamers.

Trails to the Tanana.—The upper part of the Tanana can easily be reached from the White by the route which our party took last summer. There are said to be other portages, from Ladue Creek and Katrina River, to tributaries of the Tanana. Pack trains have been brought to the Tanana from the Copper River by both the Suslota and the Mentasta passes, and neither route offers any serious difficulties. From the Sushitna the Tanana can be reached by both the Delta and the Cantwell river valleys. The best-known route to the Tanana is by the trail from Fortymile Creek, which has long been used by the Indians. It runs from the Ketchumstock Indian village to Tanana River over a low rolling country, and the distance is estimated at

40 miles. Several routes have been followed by pack trains from this part of the Tanana to Dawson and to the Fortymile district. A pack-train route was also established last summer from Circle City to the Tanana by way of Birch Creek; this trail reaches the Tanana near the Salchacket River, and is indicated on the accompanying map (No. 9). An old Indian portage extends from the Toclat River to the Kuskokwim, a route said to have been used by traders many years ago.

Railway routes.—A railroad crossing from Chilkat Inlet to the mouth of the Nissling could easily be extended to the mouth of the White or across to the Tanana Valley. A railroad from the Copper River could cross the Mentasta Pass and from the Tanana be extended to the Fortymile district by following the route of the well-known trail. It is probable, also, that a railroad could be built at no great cost up the valley of the Chena or of the Salchacket River and, crossing into the Birch Creek district, reach the Yukon near Circle City. Of the latter route we have less definite information.

INHABITANTS.

Whites.—There were last summer possibly 50 prospectors in the entire Tanana district, and there may have been a few in the White River region, but if so we saw nothing of them. Of those on the Tanana, a few spent the winter, but many came out in the fall.

Indians.—The Indians of the White and Tanana basins, like the others of the interior of Alaska, are of Athapascan stock. Those of the White River live entirely on its southeastern tributaries, and Dr. Hayes has given some account of them in the report already cited. The Indians of the Tanana may be divided into three geographic groups: first, those living near the Tok and Tetling rivers; second, those of the Middle Tanana, living near the Volkmar and Delta rivers; and lastly, those of the lower river, whose scattered settlements extend about 170 miles up the river, to where swift water begins. The Indians of the Tanana compare very favorably with the other Indians of the interior. They are kindly, peaceful people, whose skill at certain crude handicrafts has long been known, and so far as our information goes they are trustworthy and reliable.

MARKS AND MONUMENTS ALONG THE ROUTE OF TRAVEL.

1. Straight line trail blazed by party from Snag River to head waters of Mirror Creek. Legend on tree at Snag River.
2. Spruce tree peeled and marked "U. S. G. S.," on left bank at crossing of Fortymile-Mentasta trail.
3. Spruce tree on right bank 30 feet above the river at mouth of Johnson River, blazed and marked "U. S. G. S."
4. Mound of stone and blazed tree on right bank, marked "U. S. G. S.," mouth of Delta River.
5. Cairn of stone on right bank of Tanana at foot of Bates Rapids, 200 feet

WHITE RIVER—TANANA EXPEDITION. 75

above river. Aluminum tablet; legend in tin box: "U. S. G. S., August 28, 1898, William J. Peters, Alfred H. Brooks, L. D. Gardiner, Charles Ray, H. B. Baker, A. R. Airs. End of stadia line." This monument is about 15 miles above the mouth of Cantwell River, latitude 64° 42'.

Table of approximate distances on White and Tanana rivers.

Miles.
White River:
   Mouth of White River to mouth of Snag River.............. 85
   Mouth of White River to portage from Snag River.......... 151
   Portage Snag River to Mirror Creek....................... 4
Tanana River:
   Mouth of Tanana River to head of easy navigation.......... 171
   Mouth of Tanana River to Birch Creek trail................ 231
   Mouth of Tanana River to Volkmar River.................... 281
   Mouth of Tanana River to Fortymile-Mentasta Pass trail.... 410
   Mouth of Tanana River to mouth of Mirror Creek............ 560
   Mouth of Tanana River to portage at head of Mirror Creek.. 610

Magnetic declinations, White and Tanana rivers, 1898.

Lat. (N.)	Long. (W.)	Place.	Date.	Distance (E).
° '	° '			
63 18	139 35	Mouth White River.............	June 8	34.25
63 14	140 23	Mouth Ladue Creek.............	June 15	33.25
62 52	140 13	Foot Caribou Mountain	June 27	34
62 37	141 13	Mirror Creek..................	July 29	32.25
62 40	141 27	Mouth Mirror Creek	Aug. 2	32.25
63 11	142 36	Foot Chusana Hill	Aug. 9	32.75
63 25	143 27	Fortymile-Mentasta trail........	Aug. 12	33.25
64 42	148 48	U. S. G. S. monument..........	Aug. 27	31.25

REPORT OF THE FORTYMILE EXPEDITION.[1]

By E. C. BARNARD.

ITINERARY.

The party left Seattle on April 4, on the U. S. S. *Wheeling*, and arrived in Skagway on April 11. It was found that the reindeer which were originally intended for the party were too weak to travel, so other means of transportation had to be looked for. It was also decided that the Dalton trail was impracticable at this time of year, which left a choice of two routes, one by way of Dyea and the Chilkoot Pass, and the other by way of Skagway and the White Pass. After a careful examination the White Pass route was decided on, as being less congested and not so liable to such severe snowstorms as frequently rage on the summit of the Chilkoot Pass, delaying travel for days at a time.

A contract was made for the transportation of the whole outfit to Lake Bennett at 10½ cents a pound, and the members of the party walked to this point, a distance of 40 miles, carrying only their blankets. At Lake Bennett another contract was made, and the heavy freight was forwarded to the head of Marsh Lake, a distance of 50 miles, by horse sleds, our party following with hand sleds and camping outfit. The ice was hard only in places, and on Tagish Lake sails were used on the sleds to good advantage. On April 28 we went into camp at the head of Marsh Lake, it being deemed inadvisable to attempt to proceed farther, since the ice was fast becoming dangerous.

While we were waiting for the ice to break, a large boat was built, the six Peterboro canoes which we had brought being of insufficient capacity to carry all our supplies, and sails were made for the boat and canoes. A map of Marsh Lake and vicinity was made, and a reconnaissance survey was run over to Lake Aklen and the Teslin drainage. By the 1st of May crocuses and other wild flowers were in bloom, and mosquitoes had made their appearance.

On May 27, as there was an apparently clear channel near the west bank of the lake, we loaded our boats and set sail. The next night we had been joined by over one hundred boats. The following day we narrowly escaped having our boats crushed by a jam of ice which the wind drove on the shore, but many who were camped along the lake were not so fortunate.

As there was no indication of a channel opening for the big boat, she was left with four men to follow us; and by portaging the canoes

---

[1] See map No. 10, in accompanying envelope.

and their contents for a mile, open water was again reached. After five hours of wading and pulling the canoes over the soft mud, we got past the ice field, and, setting sail, were in the mouth of the Lewes River by nightfall.

At Miles Canyon we found a number of experienced pilots who made a business of running boats through, their fee being from $20 to $50, according to size. Some of these men made as high as $500 a day. As a rule two pilots had charge of a boat, with steering oars bow and stern, while two men rowed to keep headway. However, two horse tramways were almost completed around the canyon and rapids, and, deeming it dangerous to attempt running the canyon with our heavily loaded canoes, a contract was made for portaging everything, and the outfit was all below the White Horse Rapids by 10 o'clock the next morning. We arrived at Lake Lebarge that night.

A short stop was made at Fort Selkirk, at the mouth of the Pelly River. This is one terminus of the Dalton trail; the other, which was more used during the last summer, strikes the Yukon at the Nordenskiold River above. On the 6th of June we left Mr. Peters's party at the mouth of White River, and reached Dawson, the central camp of the Klondike region, that night. This was a typical frontier town, with one main street and a population of about 5,000. Here we were joined by our big boat, which had successfully run the canyon and rapids, and then we kept on to Fortymile Post, at the mouth of Fortymile Creek. Leaving most of our outfit here, we dropped down the Yukon 40 miles to the international boundary, where the United States Coast and Geodetic Survey had already determined an astronomic position and the geodetic coordinates of several summits. From this as a base, triangulation was extended into American territory. Field work was begun on June 12. The next two weeks were spent in making a stadia survey of the Yukon River within the limits of the area shown on the accompanying map (No. 10), and in extending the triangulation control over the region. We then ascended the Yukon again to Fortymile Post. During this time our work had been delayed by extensive forest fires, which destroyed much timber during the last summer.

On June 29 we started up Fortymile Creek in three canoes, with supplies for six weeks. The ascent of the stream is not easy, and it took us three days to make the 23 miles to the boundary line. A permanent cache was made in Nugget Gulch, and packing trips were made into the country to obtain the topography. A stadia survey was also made of Fortymile Creek within the limits of the area shown on the special map No. 10. We were eighteen days on one packing trip, traveling about 150 miles.

On August 8, having completed the mapping of this district, we started down the Fortymile for the Yukon. On account of the low stage of the water and the numerous rocks, we found descending attended with more risk than ascending; but we reached Fortymile Post without accident, and, taking our remaining supplies, floated down to Eagle City, a new town in American territory on the west bank of the Yukon 12 miles from the boundary line.

At Eagle City the party divided and went in different directions, thus succeeding in finishing the map by September 1, when all work except the reading of angles on one mountain peak was completed. On account of rain and clouds, we had to ascend this peak five times before the desired angles were obtained. On September 15 we started down the river for St. Michael, where we arrived September 25, and through the courtesy of Captain Sebree, of the U. S. S. *Wheeling*, who kindly put the steamer's launch at our disposal, we were enabled to join Mr. Peters's party aboard the *Conemore*, and two hours after our arrival in St. Michael we were steaming south. We arrived in Seattle October 5.

METHODS OF WORK.

The plane-table method was followed in mapping, as the country was admirably adapted to it on account of the bare summits. The important streams, such as the Yukon River and Fortymile Creek, were mapped by stadia work and fitted in between located points. Pacing meanders were made of Seventymile, Mission, and American creeks and a portion of O'Brien Creek. The ridges were followed and plane-table stations were made on the more important points, from which a sufficient number of hill summits and forks of streams were cut in; then the drainage was sketched, giving a fairly accurate map. Elevations of important points were determined by dip angles, the datum being the transit house at Camp Davidson, estimated by the United States Coast and Geodetic Survey to be 575 feet above mean sea level. No attempt was made to draw in continuous contours on the plane table in the field, as is the rule on larger scales; but the shapes of the hills and valleys were indicated by sketch contours, and the corrected contours were drawn in in the office.

TOPOGRAPHY.

The dome-shaped hills are the striking topographic features of this section. These hills are joined by comparatively flat ridges whose gaps or lowest portions appear to have a general mean level of 3,200 feet, and are usually timbered. From the domes and ridges flat, gently sloping spurs run out, terminating with a rather sharp fall-off at the streams. The domes themselves are chiefly of granite, though some are composed of schists, or more rarely of limestone; they are from 3,500 to 4,500 feet high, with a uniformly flat top from 100 yards to one-fourth of a mile across. From the top a sharp descent of 50 to

100 feet reaches the surrounding plateau. In the northwest corner of the mapped area some ridges reach an elevation of 6,000 feet; these have been called the Glacier Mountains, on account of the beautiful examples of local (annual) glaciation here.

Fortymile Creek has cut its course deeply through an older valley, leaving benches a quarter of a mile to a mile wide, which preserve a mean elevation of about 500 feet above the present stream bed. The stream has an average fall of 8 feet to the mile, with numerous riffles. This fall permits of water being easily diverted for sluicing on the bars. Most of the smaller tributaries have some water flowing all summer. Seventymile and Mission creeks do not have the ancient benches so well marked, and the fall is somewhat greater than on Fortymile.

ROUTES.

In the Fortymile quadrangle there are three principal valleys or drainage areas, and as all the mining is carried on in these valleys and those of the tributary streams, a description of the routes followed in reaching the same may be interesting. The valleys are those of Fortymile, Seventymile, and Mission creeks.

That portion of Fortymile Creek which lies in American territory may be reached either by trail or by boat. If pack animals are not to be had, which was the case last year, and a long trip is to be made, a considerable amount of supplies must be taken and Fortymile Creek ascended by boat or canoes from its mouth. It is 23 miles to American territory, and the stream may be ascended by tracking or poling to the forks, and at times of high water up both forks as far as the map extends.

If but a short trip is to be made the ridges may be followed to advantage; and if the start is made from Fortymile Post the old Indian trail leading over to the Tanana is the best. This trail leaves the Fortymile at the mouth of Clinton Creek, 4 miles from the Yukon, which point is usually reached by boat. Then following along the ridges, it finally crosses the south fork of the Fortymile at the mouth of Franklin Creek, and, going up Franklin Creek, crosses to the Mosquito Fork and continues up it to the Tanana.

Should Eagle City be the starting point, there is a good trail which crosses the flat to American Creek about 3 miles from its mouth, and then ascends the ridge between Mission and American creeks; and once on top of the ridges, one can travel with ease in any direction. Mission and American creeks are not of sufficient size to permit of ascending in boats, and the head waters are best reached by following the ridges.

Seventymile Creek may be ascended a short distance in boats, but the head waters are more accessible from Eagle City by going up

Mission Creek and crossing through a low gap to the Seventymile drainage, or by following the ridges.

METHODS OF TRAVEL.

In regard to travel in general, Eagle City is a good center for making trips from the Yukon to the interior, and is especially well located for the distribution of supplies to the valleys, if pack animals are obtainable.

The way to travel with pack animals is to follow the ridges, which are bare and hard, affording good passage for both men and animals. The valleys, as a rule, are hard to travel, owing to the frequent occurrence of "niggerhead" marshes, and the hillsides are steep and rather brushy. The gaps in the ridges are not very low, and the descents into them are, as a rule, gradual. There is an abundance of feed for animals all over this area during the months of June, July, August, and September, and good water is readily found.

POPULATION.

Eagle City is the important town of the Upper Yukon in American territory to-day; it is finely located, just above the mouth of Mission Creek, on a flat sufficiently high to be above the flood plain of the Yukon. It now has 500 or more cabins, with a population of about 1,700. There is a post-office, and the three important companies on the Yukon—Alaska Commercial Company, North American Transportation and Trading Company, and Alaska Exploration Company—have stores there. There is also a sawmill of considerable capacity.

Seventymile City and Star City are small towns about a mile apart at the mouth of Seventymile Creek, having a total population of about 500.

On Fortymile Creek and its tributaries there are probably 300 miners; on Mission and American creeks, including Eagle City and adjacent creeks, 2,000; on Seventymile Creek and its tributaries, 700; making a total of 3,000 people in the area covered by the map.

MINING ACTIVITY.

GOLD.

Gold was discovered on Fortymile Creek in 1886, and work has been continued there ever since. Early work was done on Canyon and Nugget gulches and at Walkers Fork. During the last year mining has been successfully carried on on Napoleon, Chicken, and Franklin creeks.

American Creek produced considerable gold last year. Over the entire area numerous claims are staked, and much prospecting has been done the last winter. Some of the places where many miners are at work are Canyon Creek, Dome and Alder creeks (tributaries of O'Brien Creek), Walkers Fork, American Creek (especially on Discovery Fork), Marion and Sawpit creeks, Boundary and Castalia creeks, Cuban Gulch, and all along Seventymile Creek.

COAL.

Lignitic coal is found on American Creek about 3 miles from Eagle City. I am informed that this extends over a considerable area. Following is an analysis of a specimen of this lignite:

Analysis of lignitic coal from American Creek.

	Per cent.
Moisture in vacuo	6.75
Volatile combustible	39.13
Fixed combustible (non-coherent)	37.59
Ash (reddish)	16.53
Total	100.00
Sulphur	3.40

SODA SPRINGS.

Soda springs exist at the junction of Wood and Camp creeks, tributaries of Canyon Creek, and at the mouth of Soda Creek on the south fork of Fortymile, also on the head of Mogul Creek, a tributary of the Seventymile. These springs do not freeze over until the temperature reaches 30° or 40° below zero. A warm spring on Boundary Creek is said not to freeze at all.

CLIMATE.

The following temperature observations, taken by Mr. Ogilvie, of the Canadian Government, at Fort Cudahy, at the mouth of Fortymile Creek, give some idea of the climate.

Temperature observations at Fort Cudahy, at the mouth of Fortymile Creek.

Month.	Lowest Temperature.		Highest Temperature.		Notes.
	Day.	Degrees.	Day.	Degrees.	
Nov., 1896	17	-36.4	7	+38.5	Snowed on 5 days.
Dec., 1896	24	-55.5	14	+ 6	Snowed on 6 days.
Jan., 1897	26	-68.5	29	+ 6	Snowed on 4 days.
Feb., 1897		-34.5		+32	
Mar., 1897	20	-37.2	13	+40	Snowed on 5 days.

Temperature observations at Fort Cudahy, at the mouth of Fortymile Creek.—Continued.

Month.	Lowest Temperature.		Highest Temperature.		Notes.
	Day.	Degrees.	Day.	Degrees.	
April, 1897..	5	-38.2	16	+49	Snowed 4 days; rained 2 days.
May, 1897..	1-3	-5	18, 23	+62	Snowed 1 day; rained 4 days.
June, 1897..		32	30	80	Rained 12 days. (June, 1898, no rain.)
July, 1897..	27	33	1, 2	81	Rained 3 days. (July, 1898, rained 7 days.)
Aug., 1897.	31	27.2	14	76	Rained on 8 days. (August, 1898, rained 10 days.)
Sep., 1897..	30	4.8	17	63	Snowed 2 days; rained 2 days.
Oct., 1897...	6	1	10, 15	51	Rained 1 day.
Nov., 1897..	29	-38	2	+22.5	Snowed 6 days.

Ice on Fortymile Creek broke up on May 11, 1897; Yukon River broke up on the 17th and ran thickly with ice until the 23d.

Ice on the river on September 28, 1897, which ran until October 13, when the river cleared and ran clear until October 29; but Fortymile remained more or less frozen.

Ice set in the Yukon on November 5, 1897.

The summers are comparatively dry, the snow going off in May and falling to remain in October. The average temperatures during the summer months of June, July, August, and September are 30° to 40° minimum, and 70° to 80° maximum.

TIMBER.

Spruce is the prevailing timber, and reaches a diameter of 20 inches, the best being found on the flats and in the heads of the gulches. There is also some white birch and some poplar on the flats and low hills. The timber line is at an altitude of about 3,000 feet.

FOOD RESOURCES.

Small garden vegetables, such as beets, cabbage, lettuce, radishes, and even potatoes, have been raised at Fortymile Creek. Barley and oats grow well, but we are reliably informed that they will not ripen, though they would make good fodder for stock.

As for game, the moose, caribou, black and brown bear, and mountain goat are found in this section, and the bighorn or mountain sheep is said to live on the east side of the Yukon. On the bare hill summits numerous ptarmigan are found. The moose are rather scarce and as a rule are found in the thick brush along the streams.

The caribou are quite numerous and are found in small bands on the ridges during the summer. In winter they herd, and are said to migrate. They are easily killed, since they are curious and will approach close, and large numbers are killed every winter by the Indians. The remains of a brush fence that extended for several miles were found by our party. There were openings at intervals in this fence, and some rawhide lariats cached near one of these openings made it clear to us that in the openings nooses were set and the caribou trapped.

Grayling are found in most of the streams, and in the deep pools of even small ones. King and dog salmon ascend the Yukon in July, August, and September. They are caught in great numbers by the Indians and dried for winter use and for dog feed. The king salmon is especially good eating, although not very plentiful; but even the dog salmon is a grateful change from bacon.

PART II.—GENERAL INFORMATION CONCERNING THE TERRITORY; BY GEOGRAPHIC PROVINCES.

THE YUKON DISTRICT[1].

By ALFRED H. BROOKS.

GEOGRAPHY.

LIMITS OF THE YUKON DRAINAGE BASIN.

An examination of the map of Alaska will show a crescent-like bend of the coast along the Gulf of Alaska, and a study of the dominant mountain chains will show that they too experience this marked change in direction, which amounts almost to a right angle. The Yukon, where it touches the Arctic Circle, makes a similar southwest bend, so that its drainage basin includes a large irregular-shaped area lying in part in Alaska and in part in British Northwest Territory. The chief of the Yukon tributaries are the Koyukuk, the Tanana, the Porcupine, the White, the Pelly, and the Lewes; the two last-named rivers unite to form the Yukon proper.

The head waters of the Lewes lie but 25 miles distant from the coast at Lynn Canal. On the southeast, east, and northeast the limits of the Yukon drainage basin lie first in a low divide in the interior

---

[1] In this brief summary it would be inexpedient to make detailed references for all the facts cited from various authors. Those interested in the geology and geography of the region I would refer to the following publications, from which many data for this sketch were obtained:
Alaska and Its Resources, by Wm. H. Dall, 1870.
Report on an exploration in the Yukon district, N. W. T., and adjacent northern portion of British Columbia, by George M. Dawson: Ann. Rept. Geol. Nat. Hist. Survey Canada, 1887, Part B.
On the late physiographical geology of the Rocky Mountain region in Canada, with special references to changes of elevation and to the history of the Glacial period, by G. M. Dawson: Trans. Royal Soc. Canada, Vol. VIII, 1890.
Report on an exploration in the Yukon and Mackenzie basins, N. W. T., by R. G. McConnell: Ann. Rept. Geol. Nat. Hist. Survey Canada, Vol. IV, 1888-89, Part D.
(The Publications of the Canadian Geological Survey may be ordered through The Scientific Publishing Company, 27 Park Place, New York; also directly from Librarian Geological Survey Office, Ottawa.)
The Klondike Official Guide, prepared by Wm. Ogilvie, Dominion Land Surveyor and Explorer, published by authority of the Department of the Interior of the Dominion of Canada, 1898.
Notes on the surface geology of Alaska, by I. C. Russell: Bull. Geol. Soc. America, Vol. 1, 1889, pp. 99-162.
An expedition through the Yukon district, by C. Willard Hayes: Nat. Geog. Mag., Vol. IV, 1892, pp. 117-162.
The Yukon district, by C. Willard Hayes: Jour. School Geog., Vol. I, 1894, pp. 236-241, 269-274.
Geology of the Yukon gold district, by Josiah Edward Spurr; with an introductory chapter on the history and condition of the district to 1897, by Harold Beach Goodrich: Eighteenth Ann. Rept. U. S. Geol. Survey, Part III, 1898, pp. 87-392.
Die geologischen Verhältnisse der Goldlagerstätten des Klondikegebietes, von Dr. Otto Nordenskjöld, Upsala: Zeitschrift für praktische Geologie, March, 1899, p. 71.

plateau, where the Yukon waters are separated from those of the Stikine and a branch of the Mackenzie, and then, farther north, in the northern extension of the Rocky Mountains.

The Rocky Mountains continue to near the Arctic Ocean and then make an abrupt turn to the west, parallel to that coast, forming the Romanzof, Davidson, and DeLong mountains, in which lies the Arctic-Yukon watershed. Farther west this divide is little explored, but the mountains decline in elevation and connect with those which separate the Yukon and Kotzebue Sound waters.

On the southwest side of the Yukon Basin the Coast Range in its northwestern extension merges into the interior plateau, while the great mountain mass of the St. Elias Range forms the barrier between the coast and the interior, and in part also the watershed. This range continues northward to the head of White River, beyond which the divide is more sharply defined by the Nutzotin Mountains and the Alaskan Range, which separate the Yukon waters from those of the Copper and Sushitna rivers. In about longitude 150° the Alaskan Range makes a decided bend to the southwest, and from this point on the Yukon Basin is confined by a minor range lying between the Tanana and the Kuskokwim.

YUKON PLATEAU.

The Upper Yukon Basin is an undulating dissected plateau which slopes to the northwest. On the Lower White River the summits marking the dissected plateau stand at about 4,800 feet. The top of Mount Chusana, on the Middle Tanana, reaches the level of the old plateau surface, which here has an elevation of 3,200 feet, while in the Fortymile district it is probably about 3,500 feet. The Mentasta Pass, which marks a decided break in the mountain range and is a broad, flat depression, probably indicates the same erosion surface, with an elevation of 3,000 to 4,000 feet. Remnants of the old plateau have been preserved in a series of flat-topped mountains which extend along the Yukon and Tanana divide; these attain, in the Birch Creek district, heights of 3,500 to 4,000 feet.

North of the Yukon our topographic data are very meager. A low, rather even-crested mountain range called Yukon Hills, with an elevation of 1,000 to 2,000 feet, separates the Yukon and Koyukuk valleys. The Snow Mountains, described by Allen, have an E.-W. trend and seem to rise above a general flat-topped upland surface.

RIVERS OF THE YUKON BASIN.

In this account of the rivers of the Yukon Basin, because of limited space, only the larger ones have been included. Under the description of the gold districts a brief account will be found of some of the smaller rivers and creeks which are important because of their mineral wealth.

The main Yukon River.—In its upper course, from Fort Selkirk to Circle City, the Yukon Valley is cut in the upland plateau already described, and has a width of from 1 to 2 miles. The sides of the valley rise abruptly from the river, while terraces and bluffs are prominent features of the topography. Near the international boundary the valley contracts to about half a mile, and the valley walls rise rather precipitously to an elevation of 1,500 feet above the river. From Circle City to the Ramparts the river flows through what is known as the Yukon Flats. This is a broad lowland extending from the Rampart and Tanana mountains to the range of hills separating the Koyukuk and the Yukon, and up the Porcupine to the lower ramparts of that river; it has a length of nearly 200 miles and a width averaging about 100 miles. Within this lowland the Yukon is usually broad and separated into many channels.

Below the flats the Yukon traverses the Rampart Mountains for a distance of about 50 miles; here its valley is in many places contracted to less than half a mile, while its walls rise precipitously, and the waters are confined to a single channel.

Below the mouth of the Tanana the Yukon has typically a broad valley, meanders over a wide flood plain, and divides into several channels. The delta is about 75 miles long and 50 miles wide, and the region about it is flat and treeless, with occasional low mountains or hills, usually isolated and forming no definite ranges.

Koyukuk River.—The Koyukuk River joins the Yukon from the northwest, about 450 miles from its mouth, and is one of its largest tributaries. It flows in a generally southwest direction and has a large drainage basin. Lieutenant Zagoskin, of the Russian Navy, explored this river for about 50 miles in 1842; but for nearly half a century afterwards it was known only through the reports of Indians and traders. In 1885 Lieut. H. T. Allen made an exploration as far as the sixty-seventh degree of latitude, and to the present day his map and report afford the only accurate information we have of this river.[1]

The Lower Koyukuk, according to Allen, has an exceedingly tortuous course for 200 miles above its mouth. The only large tributary in this part of the river is the Husliakakat, said to be a hundred yards wide at its mouth. This tributary heads near the Selawik River, which flows into Kotzebue Sound, and with which it is probably connected by trail. Near its mouth the Koyukuk is about 500 yards wide and has a current of about 3 miles an hour. The upper river is straighter and is for the most part confined to one channel, with occasional islands. Allen reports that in the portions of the river visted by him the bottom is hard, that there are no quicksands, and that the current is not over 4 miles an hour.

---

[1] Report of an expedition to the Copper, Tanana, and Koyukuk rivers in the Territory of Alaska, by Lieut. Henry T. Allen, U. S. A.; Senate Documents, 1887.

Above the sixty-seventh degree of latitude no surveys have been made of the Koyukuk. The sketch of this portion of the river shown on the accompanying map of Alaska (No. 1) was made from the reports of prospectors, and while the general features are correct, it can not be compared in accuracy to the results of even the roughest surveys which have been made elsewhere in the Territory. We know that the Upper Koyukuk drains a large basin and that in its upper course it is divided into several streams of nearly equal size.

Tanana River.—The Tanana River has its source near the head waters of the White and also of the Copper River, and is one of the most important tributaries of the Yukon. It has a general northwesterly course and joins the Yukon some 800 miles above its mouth. As a special report in this publication (p. 64) is devoted to this and the White River, the reader is referred to that for a more detailed account.

Porcupine River.—The Porcupine, one of the largest tributaries of the Yukon, joins it near the Arctic Circle, in the Yukon Flats. It has long been known to the British fur traders, who used it as a highway to Fort Yukon, at its mouth, which was established in 1847. In 1888 Mr. R. J. McConnell, of the Canadian Geological Survey, crossed from the Mackenzie waters to the Porcupine by way of the Peel River portage.[1] McConnell followed the river down to its mouth, but did not carry his surveys much beyond the international boundary. In the same year Mr. William Ogilvie, Dominion Land Surveyor, crossed from the Yukon to the head waters of the Porcupine, and again from the Porcupine to the Mackenzie, by the McDougall Pass.[2] In 1889 a United States Coast and Geodetic Survey party, in charge of Mr. J. H. Turner, ascended the Porcupine about 50 miles by steamer, and continued in small boats to the one hundred and forty-first meridian, where they wintered, for the purpose of establishing the international boundary by astronomic observations.[3] In March, 1890, a small party led by Mr. Turner crossed to the Arctic coast, with dog teams, along the international boundary line.

The Porcupine heads in about latitude 65° 30', within 75 miles of the Yukon; it flows northeast to the Rocky Mountain chain, and then bends sharply southwest, making a total length of about 500 miles to its junction with the Yukon. It has its source in, and for the first hundred miles of its course flows through, the Mammoth Mountains, which rise from 2,000 to 3,000 feet above the river level; below the mountains it enters a rolling upland region, which is here and there interrupted by mountains, such as the Old Crow Range. The Porcupine is a clear-water stream, with comparatively slow current;

---
[1] Report of the exploration in the Yukon and Mackenzie basins, N. W. T.: Ann. Rept. Geol. Nat. Hist. Survey Canada, Vol. IV, 1888–89, Part D.
[2] Exploratory Survey of part of the Lewes, Tatonduc, Bell, Trout, Peel, and Mackenzie rivers; Report to Minister of Interior, Ottawa, 1890.
[3] U. S. Coast and Geod. Survey Rept., Part I, 1891, p. 87.

in the Ramparts the current is from 3 to 5 miles an hour, but elsewhere on the river, as far up as the Mackenzie portage, it seldom exceeds 2 miles.

White River.—The head waters of the White River lie near those of the Tanana and Copper rivers. It is about 200 miles long. Rising in Alaskan Territory, it crosses the international boundary and empties into the Yukon about 100 miles above Dawson. A special report on the White and Tanana rivers, in this publication (p. 64), contains more detailed information.

Pelly and Lewes rivers.—The junction of these two rivers in about latitude 63° 45' forms the Yukon. The Pelly River has its source opposite the head waters of the Stikine and Liard rivers, and has a northwest trend; the Lewes rises in the Coast Range, and has a northerly course. The chief tributary of the Lewes—the Teslin (Hootalinqua)—has its source in Lake Teslin (Aklen). The valleys of both the Pelly and the Lewes are cut into the upland plateau region, while their drainage basins contain a number of peaks and mountain ranges rising above this plateau. Their entire drainage basins are within Canadian territory.

GEOLOGY.

ROCK FORMATIONS.

Within the Yukon district are found formations varying in age from what are probably Archean to the unconsolidated Pleistocene beds of the Yukon silts, while igneous rocks occur in great abundance and variety. Just as the most striking feature of the topography is the great southwesterly bend which the mountain ranges take in central Alaska, so the rocks have a corresponding change in the direction of their strike; south of the great bend of the Yukon the prevailing strike is NW.-SE., while on the Lower Yukon it is NE.-SW.

In the southeastern part of the basin, which will be considered first, while the NW.-SE. structure dominates, it is not the only line of deformation, since in the Birch Creek and Fortymile districts a system of cross folding exists which is nearly at right angles to the general strike.

In crossing by way of the Chilkoot or White Pass from Lynn Canal, the broad belt of granite which forms the Coast Range is traversed. This granite mass is flanked on the eastward side by the slates and schists which overlie it. While typically massive, the granite is locally altered into a mica-schist, is cut by basic dikes, and volcanic rocks are found associated with it. Succeeding the granite, inland, is a series of more or less altered Paleozoic rocks whose general succession is probably as follows: The oldest beds are a series of quartzites and quartz-schists overlain by white crystalline limestone, and in their turn succeeded by black slates and conglomerates with which considerable tuffaceous material is associated. This entire series is closely folded and includes intrusive rocks; it probably continues northward along the Lewes to about the mouth of the Big Salmon River. Along Lake Lebarge there are several areas of Cretaceous rocks, and below the Big Salmon is another such area, while near Fort Selkirk occurs a mass of granite which, together with the associated metamorphic schists, probably belongs to a pre-Paleozoic series.

In the gold districts of the Middle Yukon a basal granite is succeeded by the Birch Creek series, made up chiefly of quartz-schists and quartzites; and these pass above into a white crystalline limestone formation, named the Fortymile series. The Rampart rocks, characterized by a greenish color and a preponderance of volcanic material, overlie these unconformably and are probably Lower Paleozoic in age. The two older formations are more altered than the younger, but all three have suffered considerable deformation, and igneous intrusions are abundant. All contain mineralized quartz veins and shear zones. Spurr also describes some younger Paleozoic rocks, as well as Cretaceous and Tertiary beds, in the region studied by him.

From the foregoing descriptions of the Fortymile and Birch Creek district and the account of the geology of the Tanana region which will be found in the special report, the following facts are made clear: A basal gneissoid and granitic series which is found along the Tanana River, lying chiefly to the east of it and crossing the Lower White, is probably coextensive with the granite masses found at Fort Selkirk and on the Pelly. To the north this basal complex is succeeded by the Birch Creek, the Fortymile, and the Rampart series, together with the younger formations. On the south the granite is overlain by the Tanana schists, probably of the same age as one of the series described by Spurr. Along the Upper White River these Tanana schists are succeeded by the Upper Paleozoic beds called the Wellesley formation.

The region between the Yukon and the Rocky Mountains has not been investigated, but McConnell has shown that where the Liard cuts the range and where he traversed it in crossing from the Mackenzie to the Porcupine, it is made up of closely folded Paleozoic and Mesozoic rocks. The basins of Tertiary rocks have already been referred to in this part of the district. Compared with the older rocks their deformation has been very slight.

North of the Yukon gold-bearing rocks have been reported from the Upper Koyukuk, and the range of mountains bounding the basin on the north is believed to be the extension of the Rockies. On the Lower Yukon are found Cretaceous and Tertiary rocks having a NE.-SW. strike. The most important of the formations is the Kenai series, because of the coal beds which it carries.

GLACIATION.

The northern limit of glaciation, as determined by the investigations of Dawson, Russell, and Hayes, crosses the Pelly near the mouth of the McMillan River, the Lewes near the Big Salmon River, and the White near the mouth of the Donjek River. The Tanana River as far as explored by me was found to be beyond the line of general glaciation. North of this limit local glaciation has occurred on some of the higher mountains. After the retreat of the ice the region stood at a much lower level, and the silts and gravels were deposited probably in part in fresh-water lakes and in part as littoral marine sediments in estuaries.[1] The subsequent elevation and dissection of these deposits produced the terraces and bluffs which are such striking features of the topography along most of the rivers.

RECENT VOLCANIC ACTIVITY.

Doctors Dawson and Hayes have described the white volcanic ash which forms the surface bed over large areas in the region of the White River, the lower courses of the Pelly and Lewes, and the Upper Tanana. At several localities recent effusions of a basic volcanic rock have taken place. Such a one is found at Miles Canyon and White Horse Rapids, where the river has cut a narrow canyon through a lava flow which at a time not far remote obstructed the valley.

MINERAL RESOURCES.

GOLD.

Several of the formations which are more or less widely distributed in the Yukon Basin contain disseminated gold, which has two distinct modes of occurrence; one is in quartz veins and the other along what are called shear zones. The material of the mineralized quartz veins has come from below, and the following minerals are likely to occur in it: free gold, pyrite, galena, and sometimes hematite. The shear zones are belts along which the rock has been crushed and squeezed; into these the mineralizing solutions have penetrated and deposited gold, iron and copper pyrite, galena, and various other minerals, usually accompanied by quartz and calcite. By the disintegration of such mineralized rocks the gold becomes loose or placer gold, which may be found in place or may have been transported and then laid down again in sand and gravel. If such a deposit of sand and gravel occurs in a region in which an uplift takes place, the streams will finally cut a new channel through it and in time the remnants of the bed will appear on the side of the valley as terraces or benches. These

---
[1] See reports of Dawson, Russell, Hayes, and Spurr (p. 85 of this report, footnote).

old terraces, which are now much worked in some portions of the Yukon district, are the so-called bench claims.

In classifying gold deposits we have the two general heads of vein deposits and placer deposits. The latter may be subdivided into gulch diggings, bar diggings, and bench diggings. The first includes the gold found along creek and small stream beds, and the bar diggings are those in the river bars, while the bench diggings have already been described. The first discoveries of gold on the Yukon were made in the bar diggings; then the gulch diggings came into prominence; while the benches, except perhaps the very lowest, have been only recently investigated. As yet there are no working vein mines in the district, but many claims have been staked, and it is probable that mining machinery will be taken in this spring.

The geologic descriptions embraced in the following notes on gold deposits lying on or near the Yukon River were obtained largely from Spurr's report in the Eighteenth Annual Report of the Survey, Part III, to which the reader is referred for more detailed information.

Gold Mountain.—In ascending the Yukon from its mouth this point is the first where gold is known to have been found. It is situated on the right bank about 35 miles below the mouth of the Tanana. It is a quartz vein containing some gold, along which a drift was run several years ago.

Mynook district.—Under this heading are grouped a series of creeks entering the Yukon within the Rampart Mountains, the most important of which is Little Mynook Creek; other creeks of the district are known as Big Mynook, Mike Hess, and Russian. The center of distribution is Rampart City, located on the Yukon at the mouth of the Big Mynook. The richest claims that have been found in the district are numbers 6, 7, 8, and 9 "above discovery" on the Little Mynook. The gold from these claims is coarse and very pure. The Mynook drainage basin is said to have been more or less prospected to its head waters, and some claims have been located on the Tanana side of the divide. Bench claims were beginning to draw attention last season, and a rich bar digging, called Idaho Bar, was reported.

Birch Creek district.—This embraces the drainage basin of Birch Creek, which enters the Yukon from the east about 100 miles below the big bend. For 100 miles or more from its mouth Birch Creek meanders through the Yukon Flats, and the gold diggings are found above the flats. The distributing point for the district is Circle City, which is connected with Birch Creek by an 8-mile trail. The entire drainage basin is underlain by the Birch Creek schists. Two systems of dikes (igneous rocks) cut through the schists; one is made up of massive granitic rocks—i. e., granites that have not been squeezed—and the other embraces granitic and dioritic rocks in which schistosity has been developed. The thickness of gravel above the pay streak varies considerably, running from 3 to 12 feet and over on the different creeks of the district. Among the important creeks of the Birch Creek drainage basin are Mastodon, Miller, and Deadwood.

Seventymile district.—The Seventymile River enters the Yukon from the south about 70 miles below the international boundary. Gold discoveries were reported in its drainage basin last summer. The diggings may be reached by ascending the river from its mouth, where there are two settlements, named respectively Star City and Seventymile, or by trail from Eagle City. Some account of this river will be found in Barnard's report in this publication (p. 76). Four or five miles below Seventymile on the Yukon are a number of small creeks flowing from the south. Among these are Trout, Fourth of July, and Dewey, on which gold is said to have been found. Small settlements have sprung up at the mouths of many of these creeks.

Mission Creek district.—Mission Creek joins the Yukon from the south about 8 miles below the international boundary, and is easily accessible from Eagle City, which is located at its mouth. According to Spurr, the gold of this creek as well as of its chief tributary, American Creek, is derived from the Rampart schists. Barnard's report will be found to contain further details.

Fortymile district.—This is the oldest, and up to the time of the discovery of the Klondike the most important, district in the region. Fortymile River enters the Yukon some 50 miles above the international boundary, and the mouth and lower part of the river are therefore in Canadian territory. The gold-bearing portion of the district is chiefly on the Alaskan side of the line. The district may be reached by ascending the river from Fortymile Post at its mouth, or by an all-American route by trail from Eagle City. Spurr has shown that in this district an old granite mass is flanked on either side by by the younger gold-bearing Birch Creek series, which are succeeded by the Fortymile series, also gold-bearing. For further details the reader is referred to Spurr's[1] and Barnard's reports.

Sixtymile district.—This district is included in the drainage basin of Sixtymile River, which heads in Alaskan territory and after crossing the international boundary enters the Yukon about 50 miles above Dawson. As the swift current of the river makes it difficult of ascent, the head waters are usually reached by trail from Fortymile. Geologically considered, as far as this district has been studied, it is a portion of the Fortymile region.

Koyukuk district.—The Koyukuk River has already been described as one of the chief tributaries of the Yukon. Gold has been reported from various points on the river, but the important deposits seem to be above Peavy, which can be reached by steamer from the

---

[1] Eighteenth Ann. Rept., Part III, 1898, p. 317 et seq.

mouth, though the navigation of the last hundred miles is said to be difficult on account of sand-bars. Above Peavy different forks of the river are navigable for some distance farther by very light-draft steamers.

There are three portage routes to the Koyukuk from the Yukon. The first is made by ascending the Tozikakat and making a day's portage to the Konooteua River, a branch of the Koyukuk; the second is from the Dall River to the Jim River, a branch of the south fork of the Koyukuk; the third is by way of the Gens de Large River to the south fork of the Koyukuk. Indian portages are said to exist from some of the northern tributaries of the Koyukuk to the Kowak.

The gold on the Koyukuk is said to be derived from a conglomerate. Tramway Bar is the best-known digging, but there are many other localities from which workable gold is reported. The North American Trading and Transportation Company has a post at Peavy, and the Alaska Commercial Company has one at the mouth of the Allenkakat River.

Porcupine River.—Vague rumors have been spread about the finding of profitable gold deposits on this river. From what is known of the geology, however, they would seem to be entirely without foundation.

Klondike district.—The name "Klondike" is probably better known throughout the world than any other geographic name on the continent. To those not familiar with the region the name is generally used as a synonym for any part of the gold-bearing regions of western Canada and Alaska, while in fact it is the name of a comparatively insignificant river in British Northwest Territory.

The Klondike gold district, strictly defined, embraces a portion of the drainage basins of the Klondike and Indian rivers, which enter the Yukon from the east near the sixty-fourth degree of latitude; the district thus probably includes an area of about 350 square miles. The Klondike is a shallow stream, flowing in a rather broad valley, and has a width of a hundred yards at its mouth. There have been no surveys made of the entire river, but it is estimated to be about 120 miles long. For the first 30 miles of its course it is bounded on either side by hills of rounded outline and comparatively moderate relief; beyond this the river forks in a lowland, and the two most northerly forks rise in the foothills of the Rocky Mountains. Terraces or benches are found on the Klondike and on its tributaries. Indian River is of smaller size, but has a similar character; and between these two rivers lies a mountain mass usually called The Dome. The Canadian geologists have not yet published the results of their investigations, but it is known that the bed rocks of the region are of schistose character, and they are probably of the same age as those farther west in Alaska, already described.

The important gold-producing creeks of the region, as far as now known, have their sources in The Dome. Those tributary to the Klondike flow in a northwesterly direction, while the tributaries of Indian River flow southwest. It is stated that the pay streak lies on or near bed rock, and that the overlying deposit of gravel and fine material sometimes has a thickness of 40 feet. Bench as well as gulch claims are worked in this district.

The distributing point for this district is Dawson, whence the gold diggings can be reached by trail.

Other gold districts of British Northwest Territory.—For reports on these regions the reader is referred to the publications of the Geological Survey of Canada, already cited. Gold has been reported as occurring in paying quantities at various localities on the Pelly and Lewes rivers and their tributaries.

Atlin Lake district.—This district lies entirely within British Columbia, near the lake from which it derives its name. Attention was first drawn to the region by rumors of valuable gold finds last August, and a rush took place in the late summer. The discovery was made on Pine Creek, which flows into Lake Atlin from the east. Of the geology we know only that the bed rock is a slate or schist and that it is possibly the equivalent of the Paleozoic slates on the upper end of Marsh Lake, which are known to be more or less mineralized. Reports from this district have all been favorable. The local distributing point is Atlin City, situated on the lake. Steamboats from Lake Bennett run to a branch of Taku Arm, from which a portage of about 5 miles is made to Atlin Lake; or an overland trail about 30 miles in length leads from the end of the White Pass Railroad to Taku Arm.

Dalton trail region.—This lies between the Lewes and White rivers and north of the St. Elias Range. At present we know only that the region is drained by the Lewes, the White, and the Alsek rivers, and that it is generally a rolling country with some high mountains. There have been some gold discoveries in this region, and it is easily accessible with pack train from Chilkat Inlet.

COAL.

Coal has been found on the Lower Yukon, on several creeks emptying into the Yukon near the international boundary, and has been reported from the Koyukuk. There are rumors of valuable coal deposits on the Tanana, which the observations of our party last summer failed to verify. All coals discovered are lignites of Tertiary and Cretaceous age. Several specimens from exposures on or near the Yukon River have proved on analysis to be of low grade.

TIMBER.

The timber of the Yukon Basin, while of the utmost importance to the district, has no value for exportation. The best is found toward the head waters of the Yukon, and northward the trees decrease in size and abundance. Ogilvie reports that in the Fortymile district trees 18 inches in diameter are very scarce. According to Dawson the black pine is not found north of Fort Selkirk. The spruce is the most common tree, and so far as known is found throughout the basin. Besides the spruce the important trees are a variety of fir, the aspen, the cottonwood, and the white birch, as well as the black alder and several varieties of willow. Along the main routes of travel, but especially near the larger mining camps, the best timber has already been cut, and frequently building material has to be sought at some distance. Much timber is annually destroyed by forest fires. The timber line in the vicinity of the White River is about 3,400 feet, and in general it may be said that it decreases in altitude to the north. The delta and adjacent tundra regions of the Lower Yukon are treeless.

GAME.

The large game has been for the most part driven away from the vicinity of the mining camps and the more frequented routes of travel, while wild fowl are still abundant. In various parts of the district moose, barren-ground and woodland caribou, several varieties of bear, together with mountain goats and sheep, are found; but the fur trade has nearly ceased. One of the chief sources of food supply of the natives is the salmon, which ascend most of the tributaries of the Yukon for long distances. It seems to be definitely established that some of the hardier grains, potatoes, and certain vegetables can be brought to maturity as far north as Fort Yukon. Nearly all of the large rivers of the region have bottom lands, and often terraces, which would be suitable for agricultural purposes, and on the Lower Yukon every mission has its vegetable garden.

CLIMATE.

Elsewhere in this report (p. 133) will be found a compilation of the weather records of Alaska. In general it can be said that the interior of Alaska is a semi-arid region. The summers are short and hot (90° in the shade having been recorded at Dawson), while the winters are long and very cold. The snowfall, compared with that on the coast, is very light. Much traveling is done in the winter, even when the thermometer registers 30° or 40° below zero. The hauling of supplies and the making of long trips are much easier in winter, when dog teams can be used, than in summer.

ROUTES AND MEANS OF TRANSPORTATION.

The unprecedented rush into the Yukon district during the last two years has led to very rapid development of transportation facilities. While two years ago the prospector in this region had to carry his pack across the passes or employ unreliable Indians at high prices, to-day the same route is traversed by railways and tramways. At that time the traveler was forced to transport his lumber across the pass or whipsaw it out himself for building his boat to go down the Lewes; to-day steamers ply regularly between Dawson and the upper lakes. There are now two routes which are in general use for reaching the Yukon Basin; one is over the passes in the Coast Range to the Lewes River and down that river to the Alaskan and Klondike districts, and the other is by way of ocean steamer to St. Michael and thence up the Yukon by river steamer. The former route is much the quicker.

CHILKOOT AND WHITE PASS ROUTES.

Skagway or Dyea, on Lynn Canal, can now be reached in four or five days from Seattle by well-equipped steamers. Skagway, the terminus of the White Pass Railroad, is an enterprising city which is rapidly growing. From Dyea the trail starts over the Chilkoot Pass,[1] across which tramways are now in use. The distance from Skagway to Bennett, at the head of Lake Bennett, to which the railroad will probably be extended in the early summer, is about 40 miles; from Dyea to the same point the distance is about 28 miles.

During the open season steamers ply regularly between Bennett and the head of Miles Canyon. Tramways have been built around Miles Canyon and White Horse Rapids, and connect below the rapids with the steamers which run through to Dawson.

Those making the trip down the Lewes in rowboats or canoes will not find Miles Canyon or White Horse Rapids serious obstacles. By means of the tramway both freight and boats can easily be taken around the canyon and rapids, or the canyon can be run by boat. The White Horse Rapids were run by hundreds if not thousands of boats last season, and there have probably not been more than half a dozen accidents which resulted in the loss of life. These rapids, however, should never be attempted unless the boat is steered by one of the local pilots. Below the White Horse Rapids the only obstacle to navigation is the so-called Five Finger Rapids; but here any experienced man can take a good rowboat or canoe through, keeping the right-hand channel. The steamers running to Dawson both descend and ascend these rapids. This route is usually open for navigation from about the 1st of June to the 1st of October.

ST. MICHAEL ROUTE.

The route up the Yukon from St. Michael has long been in use, more especially for the transportation of freight. The trip to Dawson

---

[1] According to the Canadian authorities the Chilkoot Pass has an elevation of 3,000 feet and the White Pass an elevation of 2,600 feet.

usually takes a month, but the return trip is often made in a week. The Yukon is usually open for steamers from the 1st of July to the middle of September.

Reference has been made elsewhere to the navigability of different tributaries of the Yukon. The Koyukuk is navigable for steamers as far as Peavy; the Tanana under certain limiting conditions can be navigated for probably 400 to 500 miles; steamers can ascend the Porcupine probably 100 miles, and can go up the Pelly about the same distance; while the White River, on account of its very rapid current, is totally unnavigable.

DALTON TRAIL.

A pack-horse route from Haines Mission, on Lynn Canal, into the interior was established several years ago by Mr. Jack Dalton and has been much used for stock. Its season is practically limited to the time of good grass, from about the middle of May to the middle of September. The developments of the last two years make it evident that pack horses can be used to advantage in other parts of Alaska. The Dalton trail extends from Chilkat Inlet to Fort Selkirk, and a branch goes to Five Finger Rapids. From Fort Selkirk cattle and supplies are usually sent down by river, though an overland trail to Dawson is sometimes used.

TAKU, STIKINE, EDMONTON, AND COPPER RIVER ROUTES.

Besides the routes mentioned above, there are various others which have been more or less used for reaching the interior of Alaska. One of these starts at Juneau on the coast, goes up Taku Inlet, and crosses by an 80-mile portage to Lake Teslin. A modification of this route has recently been suggested for reaching the new Atlin gold district. The Stikine River route has long been used for reaching some of the British Columbia gold fields. During the recent gold excitement it was used by parties bound for the Klondike, who ascended the Stikine on the ice or by steamer to the mouth of Telegraph Creek, and thence crossed to Lake Teslin and went down the Teslin River. The so-called all-Canadian route from Edmonton has not proved a success. The routes from Copper River and from Cook Inlet are described elsewhere in this publication (pp. 26, 37, 43, 61, 105, 112, 122).

WINTER TRAVEL

The winter trip into the interior can now be made by dog teams without very grave danger or great hardship. The wise policy of the Canadian Government in establishing police stations at intervals of 30 or 40 miles between Dawson and the coast assures the traveler of finding food and shelter at no very great intervals.

POPULATION.

The population of the Yukon Basin has not been enumerated since the taking of the Eleventh Census, which gives a total of 3,912. Of these, 202 were white, 127 were of mixed blood, and the remainder were classed as Indians. These figures refer, of course, only to that portion of the Yukon territory which lies within Alaska. The natives of the Yukon Basin are Indians and Eskimos. The Eskimos are limited to the region about the mouth of the Yukon, extending up the river some hundred miles above the delta, while the great interior basin is inhabited by the Indians. Along the Lower Yukon are several tribes of Indians which have considerable Eskimo blood. The stories of the warlike Indians which are said to inhabit some of the more remote districts of the Yukon Basin are totally without foundation; both Indians and Eskimos are quiet and peaceable.

The white population of the Yukon district can at present be only roughly estimated. In 1898 probably upwards of 50,000 people entered the basin by way of the Lewes River routes and from the mouth of the Yukon, but many of these left the country without scarcely having been out of sight of the banks of the great river. There are now probably between 6,000 and 7,000 people in the Alaskan portion of the Yukon district.

Table of approximate distances on Lewes and Yukon rivers.

	Skagway.	Bennett City.	Miles Canyon.	Five Finger Rapids.	Fort Selkirk.	White River.	Dawson.	Fortymile River.	International boundary.	Circle City.	Fort Yukon.	Rampart City.	Weare.	Koyukuk River.	Anvik.	Mouth of Yukon River.	St. Michael.
Skagway to..........	0	50	160	380	440	535	615	665	705	800	945	1,185	1,265	1,465	1,665	1,915	1,985
Bennett City to......	50	0	110	330	390	485	565	615	655	810	895	1,135	1,215	1,415	1,615	1,865	1,935
Miles Canyon to.....	160	110	0	220	280	375	455	505	545	700	785	1,025	1,105	1,305	1,505	1,755	1,825
Five Finger Rapids to.	380	330	220	0	60	155	235	285	325	480	565	805	885	1,085	1,285	1,535	1,605
Fort Selkirk to.......	440	390	280	60	0	95	175	225	265	420	505	745	825	1,025	1,225	1,475	1,545
White River to.......	535	485	375	155	95	0	80	130	170	325	410	650	730	930	1,130	1,380	1,450
Dawson to...........	615	565	455	235	175	80	0	50	90	245	330	570	650	850	1,050	1,300	1,370
Fortymile River to...	665	615	505	285	225	130	50	0	40	195	280	520	600	800	1,000	1,250	1,320
Internat. boundary to	705	655	545	325	265	170	90	40	0	155	240	480	560	760	960	1,210	1,280
Circle City to........	800	810	700	480	420	325	245	195	155	0	85	325	405	605	805	1,055	1,125
Fort Yukon to........	945	895	785	565	505	410	330	280	240	85	0	240	320	520	720	970	1,040
Rampart City to.....	1,185	1,135	1,025	805	745	650	570	520	480	325	240	0	80	280	480	730	800
Weare to............	1,265	1,215	1,105	885	825	730	650	600	560	405	320	80	0	200	400	650	720
Koyukuk River to...	1,465	1,415	1,305	1,085	1,025	930	850	800	760	605	520	280	200	0	200	450	520
Anvik to.............	1,665	1,615	1,505	1,285	1,225	1,130	1,050	1,000	960	805	720	480	400	200	0	250	320
Mouth Yukon River to.	1,915	1,865	1,755	1,535	1,475	1,380	1,300	1,250	1,210	1,055	970	730	650	450	250	0	70
St. Michael to........	1,985	1,935	1,825	1,605	1,545	1,450	1,370	1,320	1,280	1,125	1,040	800	720	520	320	70	0

THE EXTREME SOUTHEASTERN COAST.

By G. H. ELDRIDGE.

In the Alexander Archipelago, which occupies the Alaskan Coast from Dixons Entrance to Cross Sound, there are many localities underlain by the Kenai series, the coal-bearing formation of Alaska, but the careful investigation by Dr. Wm. H. Dall in 1895[1] failed to discover more than seams of low-grade lignites. Considerable prospecting had been done prior to this time, but to no purpose. Most of the following notes in regard to gold in the Alexander Archipelago are based upon a report of Dr. G. F. Becker.[2]

The data which are available concerning the gold are too meager to permit any very important generalizations. There is a distinct zonal development of the deposits in the Alexander Archipelago, including Sumdum, Juneau, and Berners Bay, and the general direction of this belt is that of the schistosity of this part of the country. The great mine of this belt is the famous Alaska-Treadwell. The ores are normal gold ores, except that calcite is unusually abundant, and there is sufficient reason for connecting their genesis with eruptive phenomena. The deposits of this belt are so similar in position and character to those of British Columbia and California that, in the absence of direct evidence, they may be regarded as contemporaneous with them and probably of early Cretaceous age.

Farther westward occur the deposits near Sitka, on Baranof Island; and very possibly the source of the gold of Lituya Bay, in west longitude 137° 30', may be a prolongation of this group. The mineralizing action on Baranof Island does not appear to have been very vigorous. The island seems to be quite as old as the more easterly belt.

In the region of the Alaska-Treadwell mine the main mass of the country and the oldest rock is a carbonaceous slate of very uniform texture. The age of the slate was thought by Dr. Dawson to be very probably Triassic, from its analogy with rocks on the coast of British Columbia. There is no direct evidence as to age yet available. After the sediments had been reduced to the condition of slate, syenite was intruded into them. This intrusion was of a very irregular character, although it may be called a dike. In the Alaska-Treadwell it swells out to 450 feet in width, including, however, large "horses." To the northwest and to the southeast it narrows and is sometimes reduced

---

[1] Seventeenth Ann. Rept. U. S. Geol. Survey, Part I, 1896, p. 772.
[2] Eighteenth Ann. Rept. U. S. Geol. Survey, Part III, 1898, p. 60.

to a system of parallel dikes divided by slate. After the syenite intrusion came one of gabbro. It forms a dike a couple of hundred feet in width, and follows the northeast wall of the deposit pretty closely, though sometimes separated from it by slate. This rock has been turned to "greenstone" by the action of solutions, seemingly those attending the ore deposition.

Silver Bow Basin lies about 3 miles from Juneau, a little north of east, near the head of a stream called Gold Creek. In the hills to the southeast lies a glacier which formerly extended to the mouth of Gold Creek and built up the moraines, a part of which is now occupied by the outskirts of Juneau. This glacier excavated, or at least swept out, a considerable depression in the position of Silver Bow Basin. The depression was subsequently occupied by a lake, separated from the lower stretches of the creek by a solid rock divide. The lake beds of Silver Bow Basin are auriferous to a very considerable extent, and mining has been vigorously prosecuted. The country rock is a micaceous schist of sedimentary origin, carrying garnets.

Sheep Creek Basin lies to the southeast of Silver Bow Basin, at a distance of about 3 miles, and the two areas are separated by a divide. The direction of the mines of the two localities from one another is the same as the strike of the schistosity of the country, or as the course of Gastineau Channel. They are, in fact, on a continuous belt of quartz deposits. The rocks of the basin consist of carbonaceous and micaceous schists, whose strike is N. 40° W. and dip 70° N. Possibly there are also dikes of gabbro similar to that accompanying the Treadwell ore deposit.

At Sumdum Bay the rocks are green slate, black bituminous slate, and dikes of a massive rock, seemingly granite, but too decomposed for satisfactory study. The schists strike and dip very irregularly, from N. 45° E. to N. 70° W., and have been greatly disturbed. The main lens of ore being worked is from 5 feet in width downward. The ore consists of quartz, galena, zinc blende, pyrite, and mispickel, and is richest on the foot wall.

In the vicinity of Sitka gold occurs in quartz veins. Besides these there was reported as found last summer in Pandy Basin, several miles inland from Sitka and high up in the mountains, a shallow lake of supposedly glacial origin, where the gravel beds at the bottom show a very high content of gold. A company has been formed to drain the lake and to wash the accumulated gravels.

THE COAST FROM LYNN CANAL TO PRINCE WILLIAM SOUND.

By G. H. ELDRIDGE.

Lituya Bay.—From the beach sands north of Lituya Bay considerable gold has been taken out for some years past.

Yakutat.—Yakutat is situated on an abandoned moraine of the glaciers of which the Malaspina is now the chief; the bowlders found here are therefore those of the St. Elias Range. This morainal material carries some gold, and on the beach across from Yakutat, where the surf from the open sea comes in, the beach sands are said to pay for washing; also in some low morainal islands directly off Yakutat some gold has been profitably taken out. In the first place mentioned the surf seems to have played a part in the concentration of the gold and black sand from the morainal material, since in places where there is little surf there appears to be less concentration. Gold was discovered here in 1880.

Several hundred prospectors last summer attempted to cross from Yakutat Bay over the St. Elias Range to the Alsek River. A few of them succeeded in the attempt and explored both of the principal branches of the Alsek, finding the river to be considerably different from the representation on the map, although no data sufficient for the correction of the map were obtained. One party reached Dalton's trading post. None of the prospectors discovered any gold of importance, so far as could be learned.

Chilkat coal field.—The Chilkat coal field is situated about 12 miles north-northeast of Catalla Harbor in Controllers Bay. The mouth of this harbor is in latitude 60° 14′ 30″ N., and longitude 144° 59′ W. The place is about 9 miles east of the easternmost outlet of the Copper River. The rocks are Tertiary and supposed to be of the Kenai group, although evidences of metamorphism are found here. Leaf beds are well represented, appearing as dark beds of organic, arenaceous shale, rich in fossil flora and carbonaceous matter. Mr. F. H. Shepard, mining engineer, of Nanaimo, British Columbia, engineer for the company engaged in exploiting the field, regards these large beds of organic matter as the probable origin of the oil flows of the region.

The coal is said to have a bright black luster, conchoidal fracture, and the characteristics of semi-anthracite with the exception of hardness. The difference between these coals and those of Cook Inlet is ascribed to the presence of large bodies of igneous rock in the mountains, which has so altered both the coal and the accompanying strata as entirely to change them in physical appearance and character. The sandstones and shales are indurated and resist weathering, and the coal seams immediately contiguous to the main intrusion have become valueless, as evidenced by float specimens found well up the Chilkat River. In the field in general, alteration has been such as to raise an otherwise inferior coal to one of commercial value. The rocks in the field are conformable and the structure is monoclinal. There is no folding, only local deviation of strike. On the Chilkat River, 10 or 12 miles east of the coal field and 2 miles from the coast, is abundant float coal of the same generally high character, with an occasional specimen of the more altered variety. The river bed at this point contains evidence of near approach to the older rocks, and specimens of metamorphic quartzite, slaty rocks, and an occasional piece of granite are found. The coal seams in the Chilkat field are said to attain a maximum thickness of 27 feet, while many of them are reported from 10 to 12 feet thick and fairly clean.

The oil-bearing beds which are found in the same field as the coal are a heavy series of black shales with a few imperfect plant remains and shell casts; they are said to underlie the coal-bearing series. Both the coal-bearing series and the underlying shales must be several thousand feet thick.

In the vicinity of Cape Yakutagi (Yaktag) oil is found, but no coal. The oil occurs in the same series of shales that is mentioned above, and the overlying coal-bearing series, though not found at the coast, is thought to be farther inland. The structure here is an anticlinal fold with axis practically parallel to the coast and to the mountain range. At Cape Yakutagi, in sandstone 1,000 to 2,000 feet high on the mountain, are found well-characterized Miocene fossils. The sandstone is interbedded with impure limestone and some shales. According to Mr. Shepard, this sandstone is the reservoir of the oil, and along here the oil springs are found. Dr. Dall, on examining the fossils from the sandstone, observes that the oil here, as elsewhere on the Pacific coast, is undoubtedly derived from underlying Eocene beds.

Kayak and Little Kayak islands.—These islands are formed of folded, slightly indurated conglomerates, sandstones, and shales, overlain by gravels and sands.

Middleton Island.—On the east side of Middleton Island the beach sands are auriferous, the gold being often coarse.

THE PRINCE WILLIAM SOUND AND COPPER RIVER COUNTRY.[1]

By F. C. SCHRADER.

Topography.—Prince William Sound is a large bay at the head of the Gulf of Alaska, west of the mouth of the Copper River. A somewhat plateau-like belt of mountains about 60 miles in width—the western continuation of the St. Elias Range—separates it from the Copper River Basin on the north. The general land mass of these mountains has an elevation of about 5,000 feet and slopes gently toward the coast; its surface is studded with innumerable peaks and discontinuous or toothed ridges interspersed with local glaciers and névés, while its edges are cut by short, deep canyons, which carry off the drainage. The mountains in general break off rather abruptly both on the coastward and on the inland side. In Prince William Sound their lower reaches have been in part submerged, resulting in a drowned topography, with the mouths of the former valleys converted into fiords and inlets, which deeply indent the coast and afford excellent harborage for the largest vessels.

The Copper River breaks through the range near the coast and spreads out into a broad delta extending 30 miles to the sea. The basin of the river back of the mountains is about 80 miles in diameter, and is overlain by recent lake beds composed of silts and gravels, about 1,000 feet in thickness; the surface slopes gently from the base of the mountains toward the center of the basin, where the elevation is about 1,500 feet. Into these beds the Copper and its tributaries have cut sharp canyons to a depth of 500 to 600 feet, and are still cutting rapidly. The current is everywhere vigorous, averaging on the Copper about 7 miles an hour, while the tributaries are not safe even for small boats.

A northwest spur of the St. Elias Range extends into the basin on the east, where it terminates in the Wrangell group of rugged mountains, which reach a maximum height of more than 17,000 feet and are supposed to be mostly of volcanic origin. Between this spur and the main range on the south is the Chittyna River, the largest tributary of the Copper. The north edge of the basin at Mentasta Pass is reported to be 2,300 feet high.

Routes.—The only route which has thus far been at all practicable for getting into the Copper River country from the coast is the Valdez

---
[1] For more detailed statement the reader is referred to the special report, p. 51.

glacier trail, which crosses for a distance of 25 miles over the Valdez and Klutena glaciers. The highest part of the trail is 4,800 feet above sea level, and the whole route is totally destitute of vegetation. From the foot of the Klutena glacier the way leads down the Klutena River to Copper Center, whence the Millard trail leads north toward Mentasta Pass, the gateway to the Tanana, Fortymile, and Yukon. Other routes are being investigated.

Explorations.—Prince William Sound was first discovered by Captain Cook in 1778; it was further explored by the Spanish through Fidalgo in 1790, and by Vancouver in 1794.

In 1779 Caudra (Spanish) correctly surmised the location of the Copper; in 1783 Nagaief (Russian) discovered and ascended the Copper for a short distance; in 1794 Purtof made a passage to the second mouth of the Copper from the west side; and in 1796 an expedition under Smiloff to the Copper River was cut off by the natives.[1] Lastochin in 1798 visited the Copper with great caution.[2] In 1803 Bazanoff explored the Copper River for a short distance,[3] and sixteen years later Klimofsky made another attempt.[4] In 1843 two parties of the Russian-American Company explored the Sushitna and Copper rivers to trade with the natives.[5] In 1848 Serebranikoff, to whose researches our best knowledge of the course of the river for a long time was due, ascended the Copper, but was killed by the natives for his misconduct.[6] At the mouth of the Chittyna a single Russian remained for a few years and traded with the natives.[7] In 1882 C. G. Holt ascended the Copper as far as Taral.[8] In 1884 Capt. (then Lieut.) W. R. Abercrombie, of the United States Army, ascended the Copper as far as the Miles glacier.[9] In the same year John Bremner, a miner, ascended as far as Taral and wintered there with the natives until the spring of 1885, when he accompanied Allen.[10] During the spring and summer of 1885 Lieut. H. T. Allen, of the United States Army, made a creditable reconnaissance trip by boat and portage up the Copper from its mouth, leaving its basin northward by way of Suslota Pass.[11] In 1891 Lieut. Frederick Schwatka and Dr. C. W. Hayes, in exploring overland from Fort Selkirk to the coast, crossed the divide between the White and Copper rivers, at Scolai Pass, and descended the Nizzena, the Chittyna, and thence the

---

[1] Alaska and its Resources, by W. H. Dall, p. 317.
[2] Op. cit., p. 370.
[3] Op. cit., p. 321.
[4] Op. cit., p. 331.
[5] Bancroft's History of Alaska, p. 526.
[6] Alaska and its Resources, by Dall, pp. 272, 319.
[7] Op. cit., p. 272.
[8] Lieut. H. T. Allen's Reconnaissance in Alaska, 1885, p. 223.
[9] W. R. Abercrombie's unpublished report on the Copper River Expedition No. 2, of 1898.
[10] Lieut. H. T. Allen's Reconnaissance in Alaska, 1885, p. 23.
[11] Op. cit.

Copper to its mouth.[1] The topographic map about Scolai Pass and the Upper Chittyna by Hayes is the only one made of that district and is of value. It shows a rugged mountainous district with many local glaciers. On the Lower Copper, at the Miles glacier, the river tumbles over a belt of huge moraine bowlders and is impassable for boats, necessitating a portage of sometimes a couple of miles across moraine and glacier. During the summer of 1898 the delta of the Copper was surveyed by a party from the United States Coast and Geodetic Survey in charge of Mr. Ritter.

Native population.—The natives about Prince William Sound probably number about 300. They are mostly Aleuts, who are peaceful and have long been under missionary influence. Tatitlak, Chenega, Eyak, Nuchek, and Alaganik are their chief villages. They are not a healthy people, being frequently afflicted with pulmonary complaints.

About a dozen white men have married into the native tribes and have become residents. Two large salmon canneries, one at Orca and the other at Eyak, are operated by American companies during the summer months only. The labor they employ is mostly Chinese, imported from San Francisco for each season only. Orca is also a United States post-office, with monthly mail.

The Copper River natives probably number fewer than 300 in all. Of the Kulchana, the Tezlinas and "Sticks" (or Stephans) dwell on the Upper Copper, the Nicolai or Taral natives on the Chittyna. They are peaceful, hospitable, and honest, and aided the whites in many ways during the summer of 1898.

Prospectors and adventurers.—Led by the gold fever in 1898, it is estimated that more than 4,000 people, mostly Americans, and their outfits landed at Valdez during the spring and early summer. Of these, about 3,000 are supposed to have entered the Copper River country by way of the Valdez glacier, while several hundred attempted to ascend the Copper from its mouth. As the hardships of the country were severe and but little gold was found, the exodus began early in May and continued till late in October. Of these people probably about 300 in all remained in the Copper River country, mostly at Copper Center, during the winter of 1898-99, and a score or so at Valdez, on the coast. Application has been made for the establishment of United States post-offices at Valdez and Copper Center.

Resources.—The resources of Prince William Sound are timber, fish (such as salmon and halibut), copper ore, with some gold, and fur-bearing animals, such as the bear, wolf, fox, and seal. The business of raising blue fox for their pelts has attained considerable development.

In the Copper River country timber abounds almost throughout the

---

[1] An expedition through the Yukon district, by C. W. Hayes: Nat. Geog. Mag., May 15, 1892, Vol. II, p. 121.

basin. Some placer gold is reported to have been discovered and as being worked on the Tonsina, the Slana, and the Teikell. Apparently good gold-bearing quartz and some copper ore have been found on the Chistocheena. Judging from specimens in the possession of the natives and from reports of prospectors who have visited the region, the indications of copper on the Chittyna River are good. Bear, beaver, wolf, mountain sheep, caribou, and some moose occur in the country.

Climate and vegetation.—On Prince William Sound the climate is generally mild, with much rain and an annual snowfall of from 7 to 10 feet. Spruce, cedar, poplar, alder, and grass are of luxuriant growth.

In the Copper River country the summers are fine, much as on the Upper Yukon. Spruce, hemlock, poplar, aspen, alder, birch, and willow abound. Large areas of good pasture and hay grass, wild currants, gooseberries, raspberries, and many species of wild flowers, including roses, are common. The winters are severe, but not so cold as those of the Upper Yukon.

THE KENAI PENINSULA.[1]

By W. C. MENDENHALL.

Topography.—The northern part of the Kenai Peninsula is treated in the special report on the region between Resurrection Bay and the Tanana (p. 40). South of Resurrection Bay, on the east, the coast continues very irregular, with numerous deep fiords, the most important being Nuka Bay and Port Dick, to Cook Inlet. The shore line is everywhere abrupt, the mountains rising directly from the water, and the drainage is in almost all instances glacial.

On the Cook Inlet side, Port Graham and Kachemak Bay, near the southern end of the peninsula, and the East Foreland, farther north, are the only interruptions to a comparatively regular shore line. Kachemak Bay separates the two topographic types of the west side of the peninsula; south of the bay the scenery is alpine and irregular, while toward the north and east a low wooded plain extends as far as Turnagain Arm and the foot of the Kenai Mountains.

Inhabitants.—Along the western shore several small settlements are scattered. At English Bay, within Port Graham, a village of 100 or more Kadiak natives and a few whites and Russian creoles live by hunting and fishing. Saldovia, on Herring Bay, just south of the larger bay of Kachemak, is a village very similar in all respects. On the north shore of the entrance to Kachemak Bay is the postoffice of Homer, and scattered along the beach within the long spit known as Coal Point are buildings occupied at various times by the coal companies which have operated on the deposits here. At the mouth of the Kussilof River are some large canning establishments, and the inhabitants of the village are mostly white and Chinese employees. A few miles to the south is a cluster of native houses with perhaps a hundred inhabitants. Near the mouth of Kenai River, which enters the inlet 15 miles north of the Kussilof, the first

---

[1] The authorities from which most of the information concerning the Kenai Peninsula, the Kadiak Islands, the Alaska Peninsula, and the Aleutian Islands has been gathered, and which should be consulted by those who want much more complete accounts of these regions, their inhabitants, industries, climate, and resources, are—

Alaska and its Resources, by W H. Dall; Lee & Shepard, Boston, 1870.
Report on the coal and lignite of Alaska, by W. H. Dall: Seventeenth Ann. Rept. U. S. Geol. Survey, Part I, 1896, pp. 771-908.
Reconnaissance of the gold fields of southern Alaska, by George F. Becker: Eighteenth Ann. Rept. U. S. Geol. Survey, Part III, 1893, pp. 1-86.
Report on the Population, Industries, and Resources of Alaska, by Ivan Petroff; Tenth Census U. S., 1884.
Report on the Population and Resources of Alaska; Eleventh Census U. S., 1890.

permanent Russian settlement in Cook Inlet was established, and a stockaded fort, the redoubt St. Nicholas, was built here. At present a large salmon cannery, employing about 125 white and Chinese laborers, occupies the site, and near by is a village of 150 natives.

Geology.—The mountain range forming the central and eastern part of the peninsula is probably made up of the slates and coarser altered sedimentary rocks of the Sunrise series, described elsewhere, while the plateau of the northwestern shore is supposed to be underlain by the Tertiary beds which outcrop at Kachemak Bay and a few points farther north. More or less regularly over this Tertiary plateau unconsolidated gravels are distributed, and extend for some distance up the valleys which dissect the mountainous part of the peninsula.

Gold.—Last season gold in paying quantities was reported in veins at Port Dick, but no tests have been made of the value of the deposit. At Anchor Point, 25 miles northwest of Kachemak Bay, a concentration of gold from the bluff gravels by wave action, sufficiently rich to induce prospectors to attempt its extraction, has given employment to several miners during past seasons, and it is claimed that these gravels have yielded as high as $7 a day to the man. The most important gold fields of the peninsula are in the northern part, about Turnagain Arm, and are treated more fully in the special report (p. 47).

Coal.—The coals of Kachemak Bay and vicinity are among the most valuable and the best known in Alaska. Dr. Dall reports several seams here, varying in thickness up to 4 feet 7 inches, and the analyses which accompany his report, while usually showing excessive ash and an amount of water which classes the deposits as lignites, indicate a fair volatile and fixed carbon relation and show low sulphur. Experiments conducted by Lieutenant Schwerin in 1891 indicate for these coals about 75 per cent of the fuel value of the Nanaimo, British Columbia, product.

The attitude of the beds here and the harbor facilities are very favorable for exploitation, and the coal is used whenever the local needs demand it as a fuel. Some test shipments have been made to San Francisco and other points in the States, but in these markets the Kachemak coals are unable to compete with the better products of Puget Sound and vicinity. Port Graham also contains coal beds, but the rocks here are much folded and faulted, making extraction difficult and hazardous.

THE SUSHITNA DRAINAGE AREA.

By G. H. ELDRIDGE.

This region will be treated very briefly here, since a fuller account may be found in the special report of the Sushitna expedition in the first part of this publication (p. 15).

Topography and general features.—The Sushitna Valley is 100 miles wide by 150 long, and is inclosed by the Alaskan, Tordrillo, and Talkeetna ranges on the north, west, and east respectively. The Alaskan Range carries the highest peak in North America, Mount McKinley, 20,464 feet in elevation. The Sushitna River drains this vast watershed on the south. It has four important branches: 20 miles above the mouth the Yentna, 150 miles long, comes in from the northwest; 78 miles from the mouth the Talkeetna enters from the east; and 80 miles from the mouth the Chulitna flows in from the north. Between the delta and the mouth of the Chulitna the Sushitna maintains a width of one-half to 2 miles, with a current in the main channels of 4 to 5 miles an hour. The banks of the river in the delta region are but 5 or 6 feet above ordinary water level, but above the Yentna they range from 60 to 250 feet above the river water line. Beyond a point 5 to 10 miles above the mouth of the Chulitna the main river lies in a gorge 400 to 500 feet deep, carved in the bottom of an earlier valley from 2 to 8 miles wide, with ranges on either side rising to an elevation of 4,500 feet. This topography prevails to a point 60 or 70 miles above the mouth of the Chulitna, when the river is reported to lie in a high open country with mountains on its edges. The Chulitna drains the slopes of Mount McKinley and the adjacent portion of the Alaskan Range. At the head of two or three of its larger branches are low passes—2,700 to 4,200 feet in elevation—to the waters of the Cantwell River, a tributary of the Tanana.

Geology.—The Sushitna Valley embraces in its formations a bright-gray, moderately coarse-textured, massive or gneissoid granite; a series of slates, apparently many thousand feet thick, which constitute the chief outcrops of the Alaskan Range and its foothills; and the Kenai sandstones, shales, and interbedded coal seams, of Upper Eocene age. A conglomerate was observed on the north side of the range, consisting of a coarse sand matrix with pebbles of slate, probably from the slate series below; its age is unknown.

Mineral resources.—The mineral resources of the region traversed are gold and coal. Gold is found in placers, and was observed in every bar of the Sushitna River that was prospected for a distance of 125 miles from its mouth. Placer gold, coarser than in the bars of the Sushitna, was also found in the mountain torrents tributary to this stream running off the slates. It is highly probable that all of this placer gold is derived from mineralized quartz seams in the slates. Gold was found last season on the Chenaldna, a tributary of the Talkeetna, also rising in the slate series.

The coal is found in the Kenai formation. The beds vary in thickness from a few inches up to 16 feet, but all are badly interrupted by slate. Moreover, the coal itself is a very low grade lignite, the youngest perhaps that can be observed anywhere outside of a modern peat bog.

Agriculture.—The possibilities for extensive agricultural interests in the region bordering Cook Inlet and the Sushitna Valley are most promising. In the vicinity of Tyonek, and again at a point 20 miles up the Sushitna River, Irish potatoes, peas, turnips of the finest flavor, beets, lettuce, and radishes grow readily. In the wilds of the valleys and mountains berries abound. The soils of the valley are rich and extend to depths of 4 to 10 feet. The marsh lands are heavily grassed, those adjacent to the mountains with blue-stem, a rich grass which is well known in northern United States. The climate of the Sushitna Valley is said to be, for average years, neither dry nor wet.

Routes.—The Sushitna Valley is at present accessible only by rowboats or canoes which follow the main tributaries, but our observations led to the conclusion that trails, wagon roads, and even railways can be built with easy grade and at comparatively small expense. Moreover, the valley would furnish the most direct route to the interior of Alaska by way of the Cantwell River, which heads against the Sushitna.

THE KADIAK ISLANDS.

By W. C. MENDENHALL.

General description.—This important group lies southwest of the Kenai Peninsula, to which it is topographically and structurally related, and west of the Alaska Peninsula, being separated from the latter by the open waters of Shelikof Straits.

Beginning at the north, the principal islands are Shuyak, Afognak, Kadiak, Sitkalidak, Sitkinak, and Tugidak. Afognak and Kadiak are much the largest of these and support the greater part of the population of the group. Shuyak contains the best timber, but all of Afognak and the northern part of Kadiak are densely wooded. There is no timber whatever in the southern part of the group.

The village of Kadiak (St. Paul) is situated on the northwestern part of the island of the same name. It is a substantial town of perhaps 500 inhabitants, and has long been the trade center for this part of the Alaskan coast. Before the settlement of Sitka the Russian-American Trading Company had its headquarters here, and since the acquisition of the territory by the United States the Alaska Commercial Company has made this a base from which the local stations on Cook Inlet and the Alaska Peninsula draw their supplies. Other settlements within the group are Afognak, on Afognak Island; and Orlova, Old Harbor Village, and Karluk, on Kadiak Island. Karluk is especially important as the seat of the most important salmon-canning industry in Alaska. In 1890 eight salmon canneries were represented here, and it is estimated that 3,000,000 fish were caught.

With further development the fishing industry promises to become much more important in the Kadiak Islands than it is at present, for besides the salmon which abound in all the rivers, cod and halibut are abundant in the surrounding waters. The government has recognized the future importance of this industry by making the entire Island of Afognak a United States fishery reserve.

The inhabitants are whites, representing the commercial companies and larger enterprises; Chinese, employed in the salmon canneries; a few Russians and creoles, and the native Aleuts, probably a branch of the Eskimo family. The latter still engage in sea-otter hunting, sealing, and trapping, but also in many instances cultivate considerable gardens and raise cattle.

Geology and mineral resources.—Tertiary beds are reported to occur in many places on the islands. The Russian authorities give vague descriptions of several localities about the middle of Kadiak Island itself where plant-bearing sediments occur. Dr. Becker and Mr. Purington collected samples of coal near the beach at Red River, Kadiak; and in the Eleventh Census report coal of good quality but inconvenient of access is stated as occurring at Sitkinak Island. Besides these coal-bearing rocks, an older series, apparently very closely related to that which forms the axis of the Kenai Peninsula, is described by Dr. Becker. Several gold properties have been located on Uyak Bay, along the west shore of Kadiak Island, in these rocks. They are described as sandstones and carbonaceous slates, and the quartz veins in which the gold occurs average probably 1 to 2 feet in width and cut across the cleavage. Associated with the gold are the sulphurets pyrite and mispickel. Free gold is easily panned from the quartz outcrops, but no definite determination of values has been made. Along the southern shore of Kadiak Island, at Portage and Ayukulik rivers, the beach gravels have been washed for the light gold which they contain. The sands carrying this gold are probably derived from the mountains several miles back from the beach; they occur in patches seldom more than an inch in thickness and a few square yards in area. The industry is as yet unimportant and does not promise well unless some cheap process, such as cyaniding, which will save all of the fine gold, can be used in its extraction. By the methods at present used a great deal of this flour gold is lost.

THE ALASKA PENINSULA AND THE ALEUTIAN ISLANDS.

By W. C. MENDENHALL.

Geography.—The Alaska Peninsula and the Aleutian Islands from Lake Iliamna to the island of Attu, and including the westernmost possessions of the United States, are geographically a unit and will be treated as such. This region is the southwestern extension of the volcanic chain west of Cook Inlet, and as the mountains are more or less completely submerged they appear as isolated islands or a continuous land mass. From Kamishak Bay the group extends southwest, gradually curving to the west and northwest, and with the Commander Islands, off the Kamchatkan coast, which belong to the Russians, it constitutes the southern boundary of Bering Sea. Topographically two types are represented—the rough volcanic backbone, lying close to the southern shore line of the peninsula, and the low tundra apron, flat and lake-covered, stretching northward from this backbone to Bristol Bay and the adjacent parts of Bering Sea. Of these two types, all of the Aleutian Islands and the southern edge of the peninsula belong to the first, while only the remainder of the peninsula is included under the second. All of the islands are mountainous, heights of more than 8,000 feet being reached. These elevations and the abundance of precipitation give conditions favorable for the production of glaciers, many of which flow down from the higher summits.

Geology.—No systematic study of the geology of this peninsular and island belt has thus far been made, although many observers have contributed limited notes on portions of the region. Chief among these is Dr. W. H. Dall, from whose publications most of the notes for this summary have been taken.

The sedimentary rocks, where found, are generally of Tertiary age, sandstones and conglomerates prevailing, with some beds of associated shale; in these Tertiary rocks occur the coal and lignite seams which have been exploited with indifferent success in many localities. The sediments are sometimes undisturbed, but are more usually folded, faulted, intruded, metamorphosed, or buried under flows—phenomena of vulcanism of later date than the sediments and continuing in fact down to the present. There seem to be fragments of an earlier sedimentary record than the Tertiary in places; e. g., on the Island of Attu, the westernmost of the Aleutians, metamorphic slates and quartzites are known, and in the middle members of the

Shumagin group of islands a similar series is reported. Jurassic rocks occur in the region of Katmai and Naknek Lake and at many other localities.

But the recent volcanic phenomena of the belt are much the most conspicuous geologic feature. The island of Bogoslof rose from the sea in 1796, and a neighboring island, called Grewingk, appeared in 1883 and has changed considerably in elevation and outline since its appearance. Akutan Island is usually active and is regarded by Dr. Dall as emitting more lava than any other volcano in the chain. The Semisopochnoi, the Four Craters, Unalaska, Unimak, Atka, Great Sitkin, and many other of the islands are the sites of historical eruptions.

The recent lavas, according to Dr. Becker, are andesites and dacites, the latter having been found only on Unga Island near the Apollo mine. Granites are reported also from the interior of this island.

Many hot springs occur throughout the peninsula and on the islands, and are undoubtedly a phase of the volcanic phenomena.

Gold.—The Apollo Consolidated, on the Island of Unga, one of the Shumagins, is the only mine west of Kadiak which has yielded any considerable amount of gold. The deposit, according to Dr. Becker, is a reticulated vein or mineralized shear zone, and stands nearly vertical, striking about N. 40° E. The country rocks are andesites and dacites, which probably overlie sediments. Besides sulphurets, calcite, native copper, and probably orthoclase occur as gangue minerals. The ore averages about $8 to the ton. There are other deposits in the immediate neighborhood, apparently along the strike of the same lead which is worked at the Apollo. Except this deposit, we have no reliable reports of gold on either the peninsula or the islands.

Coal.—Since the explorations of the Russians, coal has been known at many points in the peninsula and adjacent islands, one of the most promising localities being that of Herendeen Bay, on the northern shore of the peninsula. A 4-foot coal bed was opened here in 1890 and several hundred tons of the mineral were taken out; but after pushing the tunnel for 200 or 300 feet, the coal was cut off by a fault and persistent search failed to relocate it. Two or three hundred tons were used by the U. S. S. *Albatross*, whose engineer reported very encouragingly on its steaming qualities. At Amalik Harbor, east of Katmai Bay, three seams of impure coal, each about 18 inches thick, are known to exist, and other beds are reported on the Ugashik Lakes, at the head of the river of the same name. On the west shore of Chignik Bay a small 16-inch seam has furnished fuel for a near-by cannery, and proves to have very satisfactory steaming qualities. At Portage Bay and at Coal Bay, farther west, coal is also reported. Mining operations have been carried on in a small way at several localities in the Shumagin Islands, but the coal here is in thin beds and proves to be of poor quality. On the Aleutian Islands proper there have been no developments, but coal is reported on Unalaska and on one or two of the other islands. Tertiary rocks, which may carry lignite, occur at many points throughout the group.

Routes across the peninsula.—Three routes long in use by Russian traders and Indians converge at Katmai; two cross the peninsula by way of Naknek River and Lake, and one by way of Igagik River and Lake. Farther west Herendeen Bay, an arm of Port Moller on the Bering Sea side, is connected by easy portages with Pavlof Bay and Portage Bay on the south.

Inhabitants and industries.—The inhabitants of the region are mostly Aleuts, probably belonging to the Eskimo race. They live in small villages scattered among the islands and hidden in the numerous bays. With them are a few white traders and miners who have married native women in order to avoid the law prohibiting all except natives or white men with native wives from hunting the sea otter. Twenty years ago many an Aleut hunter lived in affluence on the income derived from the sale of sea-otter pelts; now the animal is very scarce and the industry has about disappeared; but in recent years cod and salmon fisheries have become more important and bid fair to restore in a measure the vanished prosperity. Bears, foxes, and land otters, and in places on the peninsula caribou, are important sources of food and income.

A few Russian priests still preside in their districts, and the little churches are a source of much pride to the natives.

Villages.—The village of Unalaska, on the island of the same name, is the most important town in the islands, and the westernmost post-office in the United States has been established here. Belkovsky, on the peninsula, was formerly of much importance as the center of the sea-otter trade, but has declined with the disappearance of this animal. Unga, Atka, and Attu all have populations of 100 or more.

LAKES ILIAMNA AND CLARK.

By J. E. Spurr.

These two lakes are the largest in Alaska, Lake Iliamna being half as large as Lake Ontario. As may be seen on the map (No. 1), they have the same general trend and are connected by a broad river. They are drained by the Kvichak, which is not navigable for steamers. These lakes are surrounded on nearly all sides by high mountains. Along the southeast side of both rise the volcanic peaks of the Chigmit Range, of which the chief are Mounts Iliamna and Redoubt. The Iliamna volcano was active in 1778–79, and again in 1876. The St. Augustine volcano, in the sea near by, had a violent eruption in 1883, and is still steaming. North of Lake Clark rise the peaks of the Tordrillo Range, which forms the Sushitna-Kuskokwim divide.

From Kamishak Bay a portage route extends along the valley of a small river across the mountains to Lake Iliamna. By another gap in the mountains the inhabitants of Lake Clark cross to Cook Inlet at Kustatan.

Lake Iliamna was early known to the Russians, but Lake Clark was known only by vague rumors until 1891, when Schanz and Clark visited it with dog sledges, making a map and describing the inhabitants.

Iliamna Village, on the lake of that name, is populated by half-breed Russian Eskimos, whose progenitors settled here from the Island of Kadiak. The other inhabitants of Lake Iliamna are Eskimo as far as the Nogheling River, while the inhabitants of Lake Clark are purely Indian.

A trading post for natives has been maintained for some time at Iliamna Village, the provisions being taken over the portage across the Chigmit Range. Last summer some prospecting was also done by people who reached the lake by the same route. Lake Clark, on the other hand, has been very little visited by white men.

THE NUSHAGAK RIVER.

By J. E. SPURR.

The country at the mouth of the Nushagak and for some distance up is very flat, while the upper tributaries run through a mountainous country. The Nushagak derives most of its water from the large Tikchik Lake and the Mulchatna River, which heads in the Tordrillo Range. The whole valley is densely wooded, and on the Mulchatna many very large trees are found, sometimes over 3 feet in diameter.

The region at the mouth of the Nushagak was early visited by Russians, and the traders and priests made long journeys throughout the surrounding country, of which, however, little record exists. As early as 1890 prospectors are known to have been on the Mulchatna and to have found fine gold. In 1891 Schanz and Clark, as already noted, ascended the Mulchatna and crossed to Lake Clark. The same year Greenfield passed from the Kuskokwim to Nushagak by the Holiknuk. At the mouth of the Nushagak large canneries have been established, which have a capacity of about 120,000 cases of salmon during the season of five weeks. There is a central trading post at Nushagak, and a Moravian and a Greek mission. The valley of the Nushagak and its tributaries is populated by Eskimos of the Nushagak type, and several branch trading posts are found here, which are supplied from the main station.

THE COAST FROM BRISTOL BAY TO THE YUKON.

By J. E. SPURR.

Topography.—The region around the mouth of the Kvichak River, at the head of Bristol Bay, is flat and swampy, and the shores are bluffs running up to 150 or 200 feet in height. This is also true of the shores from Nushagak as far as the western shore of Togiak Bay. At Cape Newenham the mountains which form the divide between the Togiak and the Kuskokwim come down to the coast. On the eastern shore of Kuskokwim Bay a broad strip of tundra, growing wider to the north, separates the mountains from the salt water. The shore between Kuskokwim Bay and the Yukon delta is in general comparatively low, although in places mountains of considerable height come down to the sea, especially at Cape Vancouver and at Cape Dyer.

Along this whole coast the tides are very great, especially in the funnel-shaped bays, such as Nushagak Bay, Togiak Bay, and Kuskokwim Bay. Since the water in the vicinity of the shore is very shallow these enormous tides leave great stretches of sand flats bare at ebb tide, and these often run out to sea 5 or 10 miles from the actual shore line. Outside of the flats are shoals which are never laid quite bare, so that on the whole the coast is a dangerous one.

Population.—The entire length of the coast line is fairly well populated, and all the people belong to the common Eskimo race, although to many different tribes. Those in the vicinity of Nushagak are somewhat civilized from long contact with the Russians, and later with Americans brought by the salmon-canning industry. Northwestward, however, the population becomes more primitive, till in the region between the Kuskokwim and the Yukon, and especially on Nunivak Island, they are reported to be untouched by any civilizing influence whatever.

Settlements.—The head of Bristol Bay is the scene of a great salmon-canning industry. At the mouth of the Naknek River, at Koggiung, at the mouth of the Kvichak, and especially around Nushagak, there are large canneries. The season is five weeks long, and the region of Nushagak then presents a very busy appearance. In the month of September, however, the vessels depart, carrying with them the men employed, together with the salmon which have been put up, so that during the winter only about twenty white men remain on Nushagak Bay.

At Togiak, on Togiak Bay, there is a half-breed trader who maintains a station for the natives.

Kuskokwim Bay is navigable for sea-going craft only for a few miles north of Kwinhagamut, and from this point the provisions have to be taken up as far as Bethel in a small sloop.

At Tununak, on Cape Vancouver, there is a half-breed Russian trader. A Catholic mission school was formerly established here, but did not prove successful.

Pribilof Islands.—These lie some distance southwest of the coast which has been described, in Bering Sea, and were discovered by the Russian, Pribilof, in 1776. In 1869 the islands were declared a Government reservation and a company of soldiers was stationed there. From 1870 to 1890 the islands were leased to the Alaska Commercial Company, having become very valuable on account of the immense number of seals which congregated there during the season. During the twenty years of occupancy this company paid to the Government in seal taxes nearly $6,000,000. Since 1890 the North American Commercial Company has held the lease at a higher tax. On account of being so assiduously hunted the number of seals obtained has decreased to 20,000 annually.

THE KUSKOKWIM DRAINAGE AREA.

By J. E. SPURR.

The Kuskokwim River is described at greater length in the special report of the Kuskokwim expedition in Part I of this publication (p. 28). The river is the second largest in Alaska, and the largest whose drainage area is confined to the Territory. Its length is about 700 miles to its chief source in the Tordrillo Mountains, and it is navigable for steamers for about 575 miles above Apokagamut (near the mouth).

Topography.—The main branch of the Kuskokwim rises, as stated, in the picturesque Tordrillo Range, while the east fork probably heads close to the McKinley Mountains. A short distance after leaving these ranges, however, the two chief branches unite and flow through a level country—the Kuskokwim Flats. The river keeps mostly to the north side of the flats, and the hills beyond, forming the divide between the Kuskokwim and the Tanana and Yukon, are comparatively low, timbered, and rounded. On leaving the level country, the river enters a definite mountain valley, in which it continues until past Kolmakof; these mountains also are of very moderate height. Below Kolmakof the river flows through the tundra, with mountains in the distance, especially on the east.

Routes.—The route from the Skwentna to the Kuskokwim, traversed by the United States Geological Survey party in 1898, is described in the special report (p. 37). It is also likely that a route exists from the head of the Yentna to the East Fork of the Kuskokwim. A portage trail, well known to natives, leads from the East Fork of the Kuskokwim to the Toclat River, a tributary of the Tanana. From the Tachatna River, which joins the Kuskokwim at its chief southward bend, there are portages to the Nowikakat, and also to the Tlegon, an affluent of the Innoko. From the Kuskokwim above Kolmakof a portage to Nushagak is by way of the Holiknuk River across to the Nushagak River and down that stream. From the Kuskokwim about 80 miles above Bethel a water route with a few short portages reaches the Yukon at the Holy Cross Mission. A route from Kwinhagamut and Kuskokwim Bay to Togiak Lake is described in the special report above referred to. Many other routes are known to the natives, who traverse the country in all directions.

Explorations.—In 1832 the Russian half-breed, Lukeen, crossed to the Kuskokwim by way of the Nushagak and the Holiknuk, and established a station at what was afterwards called Kolmakof. The same point was reached by Kolmakof by way of the Kuskokwim in 1836. The Upper Kuskokwim was not explored prior to the Geological Survey expedition, except possibly by prospectors who have left no record. The portage route from the Kuskokwim by way of the Holiknuk and the Nushagak was traversed by Greenfield in 1891.

Population.—A line across the country from the region of Kolmakof on the Kuskokwim to the junction of Lakes Clark and Iliamna conveniently divides the native races. Southwest of this line are the Eskimo tribes, northeast the Indian peoples. The latter are far less numerous than the Eskimos. The only white men on the Kuskokwim in 1898 were the Moravian missionaries at Bethel and one or two traders. There are trading stations at Vinasale, at Kolmakof, and at Bethel, but the last is the only reliable one. Besides the mission at Bethel, there are branch missions at Oknavigamut and Kwinhagamut.

Resources.—The Upper Kuskokwim produces a variety of valuable furs, but in no great quantity, owing to the scarcity both of game and of hunters. The lower part of the river has very little game, but a great abundance of wild fowl in season, and of salmon, of which no use has yet been made beyond feeding the native population. Some parts of this region, especially the Kuskokwim Flats, may very likely be valuable in time for raising the hardy cereals and live stock. There is also a certain amount of mineral wealth in the mountains which lie in or border the district.

FROM THE YUKON MOUTH TO POINT BARROW.

By J. E. SPURR.

Topography.—In the vicinity of St. Michael the country consists of low, bare mountains of volcanic origin. These same hills run northward parallel with the coast, being usually of only trifling height, although at a distance inland some peaks become probably 1,000 or 1,500 feet high. Golovin Bay, on the north side of Norton Sound, is shut in by two high promontories, Cape Derby and Stony Cape. The head of Golovin Bay is low, and from here a portage extends, by lakes and rivers, to Grantley Harbor. This is the best harbor in northern waters and has been long used by the whaling fleet. The whole coast from here to Cape Prince of Wales is ordinarily low and rocky, and the shore from Cape Prince of Wales to Cape Espenberg, on the southern side of Kotzebue Sound, is sandy. On Kotzebue Sound the mountains at times come quite down to the shore, especially the Mulgrave Hills at the mouth of the Noatak. From Cape Krusenstern, on the north shore of Kotzebue Sound, to Cape Lisburne, the coast is generally low and rocky, with sandy intervals. Point Hope is a long sandy tongue of land, backed by steep cliffs at its landward end. From Cape Lisburne to Point Barrow the coast is also low and rocky, with many sandy stretches.

Explorations.—The Bering Straits were first passed by the Russians in 1648, and again by Vitus Bering, in the Russian service, in 1728. Neither saw America. Captain Cook in 1778 discovered Cape Prince of Wales, and pushed a long distance northward along the coast. In 1816 von Kotzebue, a German in a Russian ship, discovered the sound which bears his name. Since that time many expeditions have sailed along these shores, especially such as in the early days were seeking a northwest passage, or those which later were engaged in Arctic exploration. For many years this whole coast has been known to whalers and to Government revenue cutters. In the winter of 1897 Lieutenants Jarvis and Bertholf, and Dr. Call, of the Revenue Marine Service, made a remarkable trip with dogs and reindeer from Cape Vancouver to Point Barrow;[1] while two mates of whalers in distress at Point Barrow, Tilton, and Walker, made long overland trips, the former reaching Katmai, on Shelikof Straits, and the latter, by way of the Arctic coast and the Mackenzie mouth, reaching Edmonton, on

---
[1] For details of this trip, which lack of space compels us to omit, the reader is referred to the forthcoming report by the Revenue Cutter Service Department.

the Canadian Pacific. Last summer many prospectors were in Kotzebue and Norton sounds.

Norton Sound.—St. Michael is an ancient and well-known trading post and requires no mention. The country within a considerable radius of St. Michael has been reserved for military purposes by the Government. There is a trading post of the Alaska Commercial Company at Unalaklik, and there are missions of the Swedish Evangelical Church at Unalaklik, at Kaugekosook, and at Golovin Bay.

Gold was long ago reported on the Fish River, which heads in Golovin Bay, but no mining was attempted. On the same river 30 miles above the mouth the Oonilak mine of silver-bearing galena was discovered long ago and the Golovin Bay Mining Company, of San Francisco, formed to work it. There was difficulty, however, in getting the ore down the shallow river to the vessel which took it to San Francisco; and, in addition to this, two vessels with all on board were lost by the company previous to 1885. In 1890 operations were suspended, owing to the report of experts that there was no continuous vein; but in 1891 work was renewed. The overflow of the Klondike rush turned prospectors into Golovin Bay, and in the summer of 1898 many claims were located on the Fish River and other streams in the district. The gold is said to be fine, but of high grade, and to be easy of access; and it is reported that there is plenty of water for sluicing. There were 300 or 400 people on Golovin Bay last summer, and last winter probably 200 prospectors spent the winter on the peninsula between Kotzebue and Norton sounds.

St. Lawrence Island.—St. Lawrence is a large island off Norton Sound, south of Bering Straits. It is comparatively barren, and is inhabited only by natives, with the exception of a few Presbyterian missionaries.

Cape Prince of Wales and vicinity.—At Port Clarence, already mentioned on account of its splendid harbor, is the Teller reindeer station, established by the Government in 1892 through the efforts of Dr. Sheldon Jackson. Mr. William A. Kjellman is the principal superintendent, and there are a number of herders imported from Lapland. There is also a reindeer station at Cape Nome, on Norton Sound. The herd increases very slowly, and a large part of it was driven to Point Barrow in 1897 to relieve the distressed whalers. Cape Prince of Wales, the westernmost point of the American mainland, is a bold promontory. Here is the Congregational mission of the American Missionary Society, in charge of W. T. Lopp, and a village of 500 or 600 Eskimos.

Kotzebue Sound.—At Kiktarak, north of Cape Blossom on Kotzebue Sound, there is a Quaker mission. The "Fort Morton" appearing on the maps does not exist and never has existed. Near Chamisso

Island, on the mainland, there is a small trading post for natives. Kotzebue Sound, as already noted, was early visited by explorers, and the ice cliffs, especially those in the vicinity of Elephant Point, where the ice plays the part of a geologic formation, have been described by many writers. The region has a fairly numerous native population, who speak the Eskimo tongue. On the north shore, however, between Cape Krusenstern and Cape Sepping, there are no natives. In the country between Norton Bay and Eschscholtz Bay there are also no inhabitants, although a village—Attemut—has been represented on maps.

During the summer of 1898 discouraging reports from the Klondike reaching the west coast, many prospectors turned their attention to unknown parts of the Territory, and a large number poured into Kotzebue Sound. Probably a thousand men prospected there during the summer, ascending also the various rivers which empty into the sound. So far as learned, however, no one had any luck, although fine gold exists on some of the streams; the conclusion was reached by most, therefore, that the region is worthless as a gold-mining country.

Point Hope to Point Barrow.—At Point Hope there is an Episcopal mission, and between Point Hope and Point Barrow are several whaling stations, the principal one 15 miles east of Point Hope and owned by Liebes & Company, of San Francisco. Between Cape Lisburne and Cape Sepping there are occasionally small Eskimo villages, and around the mission at Point Hope there is a large village. Between Icy Cape and Cape Lisburne there are no natives, and very few between Icy Cape and Point Barrow. At Cape Beaufort, and in many places thence northward to Point Belcher, coal of good quality, probably belonging to the Carboniferous period, has been reported. The climate along here is extremely bleak, large packs of floating ice being in the sea all summer. At Point Barrow and at Point Hope the lowest winter temperature is only about 30° below zero, while at Point Hope the average winter temperature is 15° below zero. At Point Barrow there is a Government relief station, designed principally for whalers.

THE KOWAK RIVER.

By J. E. SPURR.

The word Kowak seems to be a corruption of the native pronunciation, which is more nearly Kubuk or Kuvuk, the word meaning *great river*, and being the same as the Eskimo name for the Yukon, *Kwikpak*, although in a different dialect, and also the same as the Kookpuk, which enters the Arctic above Point Hope. The Kowak River was partly ascended by Lieut. John C. Cantwell, U. S. R. M., in 1884, in a small boat, and more successfully the following year, when a steam launch was used to carry the party up the lower part of the river. At about the same time Lieutenant Stoney, U. S. N., also explored the Kowak. The report of the latter officer is not yet available, so that most of our knowledge of the river comes from Cantwell's report.[1] According to this report, in twelve days from the mouth the head of boat navigation—a narrow canyon, filled with sharp-pointed rocks over which a rapid current flowed—was reached. Above this point the journey was made in a skin boat. Near the head the river splits into two branches, one coming from a lake, while the other rises in mountains across which a portage leads to the Koyukuk. This route is that always used by the Kowak Indians when going to the Koyukuk to trade.

Near the mouth of the river a short range of mountains separates the Kowak from the north branch of the Selawik. Above this for hundreds of miles the river flows in intricate channels with many sand bars, while on both sides is low, rolling tundra. Farther up the timber becomes plentiful, and then the tundra is succeeded by the mountains, where the head of boat navigation is reached. Above this the skin boat had to be towed. The shores were very rocky, with forests of spruce, pine, birch, and balm of Gilead. Between the Kowak and the Noatak the country is very mountainous, with numerous deep lakes and small rivers.

As reported by Lieutenant Cantwell, the climate of the Kowak region is remarkable for its extremes. In the middle of July the temperature rose by day as high as 96° in the shade, and seldom fell below 88°. On the 31st of July it was noted that the mosquitoes were still terribly annoying, while on the 8th of August the mountains were snow-covered and there were heavy frosts at night, after which time

---

[1] Cruise of the Corwin in the Year 1885. Washington, Government Printing Office, 1887.

there was as much hardship from the cold as there had been previously from the heat.

Along most of the route game, fish, and berries were comparatively abundant, and there were many fresh signs of bear, porcupine, and deer. Not far from the mouth of the river seams of impure clayey coal were observed; and similar lignitic coal, but of finer quality, was brought by the Indians from several of the tributaries. A remarkable feature of the Kowak is the ice cliffs, described by Cantwell. These border the river, rising from it steeply for many feet, and are composed of pure, hard ice, on top of which is a greater or less thickness of clays and silts, which in turn support a growth of trees and shrubs. The ice, therefore, appears to play the part of a geologic formation. Similar ice cliffs were early reported from Elephant Point in Eschscholtz Bay, and what appears to be the same phenomenon has been personally described to the writer by Lieut. E. P. Bertholf as occurring at the mouth of the Kookpuk River, north of Point Hope.

Cantwell's party reports having found colors of gold in nearly every part of the Kowak. Last summer (1898) many of the prospectors who sailed for Kotzebue Sound attempted to explore the Kowak, but, so far as known, with no great success. A number of steamers started up the river, but on account of the low water the farthest point reached was about 125 miles from the coast. No well-authenticated finds of gold have been reported.

THE NOATAK RIVER.

By J. E. SPURR.

Hotham Inlet was first explored and named by Captain Beechey, R. N., in 1825. In 1849 the mouth of the Noatak was observed by H. M. S. *Herald*, and was reported as being unnavigable for any distance, even for ship's boats. The river itself, so far as known, was first explored by white men in 1885, in which year S. B. McLenegan, of the Revenue Marine Service, was sent out to explore it, and succeeded in ascending nearly to the head.

Near its mouth the Noatak cuts through the Mulgrave Hills, but just before entering the inlet the river forms a delta and divides into two branches, which are about equal in volume. Back of the mountains the river runs through a flat country, in which it divides into many channels. Here the valley is bounded on both sides by parallel ranges of hills about 10 miles distant, which farther upstream become higher; at the same time the valley becomes narrower, till the river runs in deep gorges or canyons. Above this region a beautiful mountain valley, 3 to 5 miles in width, is again found; and still higher, around the head of the river, is an elevated plateau with occasional hills and vast tracts of swamp. This upper region is full of lakes, but bears no timber of any description.

The journey by Mr. McLenegan up the Noatak lasted from the 2d of July until about the 31st, the trip being made in a 3-hatch bidarky, or skin boat. Frequent rains and floods made traveling difficult, and the moorlands at the head of the river were reported at the end of July as a scene of utter desolation, being without life and covered with snow and water. The general current of the river is reported to be 10 to 12 miles an hour.

The people inhabiting the Noatak Valley are Eskimos, and were estimated by McLenegan to be about 225 in number. There are several native routes between the Kowak and the Noatak, and probably also between the Noatak and the Koyukuk. No coal was seen along the river, and no gold. Tools of jade were in use by the natives, and it was supposed that this mineral came from the mountains near by.

In 1898 a party of prospectors ascended the Noatak in rowboats 250 miles in twenty-seven days, returning in thirty hours. They found no gold. Many wild berries, especially currants, were reported along the route, and many waterfowl and ptarmigan, but there were no signs of large game.

THE COAST FROM POINT BARROW TO THE MACKENZIE.[1]

By ALFRED H. BROOKS.

On the north Alaska is bounded by the bleak Arctic coast, which for ten months in the year is locked in ice. The coast line is comparatively even, but is broken here and there by the deep embayments which mark the mouths of the larger rivers. Shallow water is usually found near the coast, and sand bars and reefs are numerous. From the international boundary westward to Point Barrow stretches a low tundra plain, covered with moss and scant grass, and dotted with numerous lakes. Through this plain meander sluggish streams and rivers. During the short summer this tundra belt is little more than a marsh. Near the stream banks are found a few stunted alders and willows, but elsewhere the coast is devoid even of these low shrubs. To the south the plain merges into a rolling country, also moss covered, and beyond these foothills is a mountain range which separates the North Arctic drainage from the rivers of Bering Sea and Kotzebue Sound. At the international boundary this range is but a few miles from the coast, with elevations of 4,000 to 7,000 feet, but in its western extension it recedes rapidly from the shore line, and decreases in elevation, so that opposite Point Barrow it is 150 miles inland and has an elevation of from 3,000 to 4,000 feet. The region is drained by numerous rivers, but only a few of these have been visited by white men. Turner River was discovered and approximately mapped by Mr. Turner; the Colville and the Ikpikpung are known through the investigations of Lieutenant Howard; and Lieutenant Ray mapped the lower course of the Mead River.

---

[1] This brief summary is based on the following publications, to which the reader is referred for further information:

Voyage from Montreal on the River St. Lawrence through the Continent of North America to the Frozen and Pacific Oceans, in the Years 1789 and 1793, by Sir Alexander Mackenzie; Philadelphia, 1802.

Narrative of a Second Expedition to the Shores of the Polar Sea in the Years 1825, 1826, and 1827, by John Franklin; Philadelphia, 1828.

Narrative of the Discoveries on the North Coast of America effected by the Officers of the Hudson Bay Company during the Years 1836 and 1839, by Thomas Simpson; London, 1843.

Narrative of the Voyage of the Blossom to the Pacific and Bering Straits, by Capt. F. W. Beechey, London, 1831.

A Personal Narrative of the Discovery of the Northwest Passage, by Alexander Armstrong; London, 1857.

Alaska and its Resources, by William H. Dall, 1870.

Report of the International Polar Expedition to Point Barrow, 1881-1883, by Lieut. P. H. Ray.

Report of J. H. Turner; United States Coast and Geodetic Survey, Part I, 1891, p. 87.

Lieutenants Stoney and Howard's reports have unfortunately not been published. A map of the region they explored, which embodies their work, was published by A. McDonald at San Francisco in 1898.

Strangely enough, this north coast of Alaska was explored long before some of the more accessible parts of the Territory were. As early as 1789 Mackenzie reached the Arctic Ocean at the mouth of the great river which bears his name. In 1826 a boat expedition in charge of Mr. Elson, sent out by Capt. F. W. Beechey, of H. M. S. *Blossom*, reached Point Barrow, and the same year Sir John Franklin pushed his way westward from the mouth of the Mackenzie to Return Reef, where he was stopped by the ice. It remained for Peter Warren Dease and Thomas Simpson to complete this line of exploration some ten years later. These men went westward from the mouth of the Mackenzie and were stopped by the ice; but Simpson continued on foot and in native boats, and on August 4, 1837, reached Point Barrow. The activity in Arctic exploration which followed the disappearance of the Sir John Franklin expedition resulted in a better knowledge of this region, because of the numerous vessels which passed its shores. Important among these was H. M. S. *Investigator*, whose crew was the first to make the Northwest Passage.

Since these early expeditions but little exploration has been done on this north coast. The Signal Service maintained a station at Point Barrow from 1881 to 1883, in charge of Lieut. P. H. Ray, and in the spring of 1886 Lieut. W. C. Howard, U. S. N., left Lieut. G. M. Stoney's winter camp on the Kowak and, with one white man and several natives, made the long trip to Point Barrow. Mr. Turner's trip from the Porcupine River to the Arctic coast along the international boundary, made in 1890, is described in the account of the Yukon district (p. 88).

A relief station for the benefit of whalers and a mission school are now maintained at Point Barrow and are annually visited by the vessels of the United States Revenue Service. The Pacific Steam Whaling Company also maintains a station at Herschel Island, to which a vessel is sent every year. The Eskimos have settlements at Point Barrow near the Colville River, and at Herschel Island and adjacent portions of the mainland. They depend on the abundant driftwood for fuel, and on the products of the sea and the wild reindeer (caribou) for food. The reindeer migrate northward in the spring and return to the mountains in the more southern parts of the Territory in the fall. The natives of the interior are said to make annual visits to the coast for trading purposes, following the reindeer northward and returning with them to the mountains again in the fall.

In 1848 the American whaler *Superior*, commanded by Captain Roys, ventured through the Bering Straits, and this example was followed by many in the succeeding years. Since then the Arctic Ocean is visited ever summer by numerous vessels employed in whaling, which pursue their calling close to the ice pack, and frequently are forced to spend the winter in this inhospitable region.

PART III.—TABULATED INFORMATION.

METEOROLOGICAL TABLES.

(Observed and compiled by Weather Bureau, United States Department of Agriculture.)

MEAN TEMPERATURE.

[In degrees Fahrenheit.]

Station.	Latitude.	Longitude.	Elevation.	January.	February.	March.	April.	May.	June.	July.	August.	September.	October.	November.	December.	Annual.	Length of record. From—	To—	Yrs.	Mos.
Coast.	° ′	° ′	*Feet.*																	
Fort Wrangell	56 30	132 28	25–35	26.2	30.8	31.6	42.7	49.3	55.3	56.2	57.5	52.3	45.9	39.5	32.8	43.0	May, 1868	Aug., 1882	7	18
Sitka	57 03	131 19	63	31.4	32.9	35.6	40.8	47.0	52.4	56.4	55.9	51.5	44.9	38.1	33.3	43.3	Jan., 1828	Dec., 1876	45	2
Sitka	57 22	131 29		34.2	33.0	37.2	41.9	46.9	51.6	54.8	56.6	52.3	45.7	30.8	36.0	44.5	April, 1881	Sept., 1887	5	18
Killisnoo	58 19	131 25		26.7	26.9	31.3	35.5	44.9	50.3	54.8	53.6	46.5	41.2	32.7	30.6	39.8	May, 1881	Dec., 1896	11	25
Juneau	58 18	132 19		27.5	24.7	33.5	40.1	47.7	53.6	56.0	55.0	49.9	42.3	31.2	29.3	40.9	May, 1883	Dec., 1896	2	54
Kadiak	57 48	152 19		30.0	28.2	32.0	36.3	43.2	49.5	54.7	55.2	50.0	42.3	34.7	30.5	40.6	Jan., 1860	April, 1896	2	31
Unalaska	53 53	166 32	18	30.0	31.9	30.4	35.6	40.9	46.3	50.6	51.9	49.5	37.6	34.7	30.1	38.7	Oct., 1827	Aug., 1898	8	54
St. Michael	63 34	161 48	10	33.5	31.9	32.6	35.5	40.4	46.3	49.6	50.3	46.0	40.4	34.6	32.8	38.3	June, 1872	May, 1886	6	31
Point Barrow	71 22	156 24		7.4	–2.3	8.9	19.9	33.1	46.3	43.6	51.9	43.9	27.6	15.6	–4.8	26.1	July, 1874	June, 1883	11	33
Unalaklik[1]	63 53	156 16	30	–17.5	–18.6	–11.8	–1.2	31.3	42.8	38.1	37.9	27.8	4.4	–6.0	–15.4	7.7	Sept., 1852	Aug., 1853	3	12
Port Clarence[3]	65 17	166 35		–10.0	1.0	4.0	11.0	33.0	40.0	50.0	46.0	41.0	19.0	9.0	3.0		Sept., 1850	Aug., 1851		
Kotzebue Sound[1]		166 20		–11.0		6.0	14.0	30.0			45.0	43.0	23.0	1.0	0.0		Oct., 1850	Jan., 1852		10
Interior.																				
Anvik	62 37	160 08		1.8	1.3	15.5	25.4	42.0			46.0	43.0	25.1	10.0	–2.1		Oct., 1882	Mar., 1891		31
Nuklukayet	65 10	152 45		–11.1	9.0	6.7	22.2	43.7					25.9	–4.6	–19.9		Aug., 1882	May, 1890		27
Fort Yukon	66 33	145 18	412	–20.5	–11.6	0.6		41.3		54.8	54.4	43.9	27.3	–7.0	–21.4		Jan., 1881	May, 1861		4
Fort Reliance	64 10	139 25		–28.7	–19.7	10.5	28.7			56.6					5.0	23.8	Sept., 1882	May, 1880		16
Internat. bound'y, Yukon River	64 41	140 55		–17.4	9.9	7.1	23.6	45.0	57.2	60.3	52.1	39.0	30.5	2.9	–15.6	22.9	Sept., 1889	June, 1891	1	10
Internat. bound'y, Porcupine River	67 25	141 00		–15.2	–15.3	6.0	6.4	41.0	51.9	56.6	48.6	28.0	20.1	–4.4	–17.4		Oct., 1889	June, 1890		9
Head waters Birch Creek	65 00	145 00	high	–5.0	–8.7	7.4	23.3	57.1	58.0				12.8	2.9	5.0	23.8	Dec., 1896	June, 1898	1	7

[1] Compiled from Coast Pilot, 1879.

EXTREMES OF TEMPERATURE—MAXIMUM.

Station.	Latitude.	Longitude.	Elevation.	January.	February.	March.	April.	May.	June.	July.	August.	September.	October.	November.	December.	Annual.	Length of record. From	To	Yrs.	Mos.
Coast.	° ′	° ′	*Feet.*	°	°	°	°	°	°	°	°	°	°	°	°	°	°			
Sitka				51	52	59	66	79	75	72	79	69	61	56	56					
Ugashik				46	49	55	59	63	83	78	86	75	56	46	46					
Unalaska				52	51	51	59	60	68	78	78	68	62	58	50					
St. Michael				44	41	43	46	57	75	75	60	69	51	42	45					
Point Barrow				21	0	24	30	43	46	51	49	41	20	24	17					
Interior.																				
Anvik				35	37	46	46	67		65	66	51	39	25						
Nuklukayet				35	38	48	52	72		79	72	51	36	17						
Fort Reliance				20	27	45	59	76			67	55	36	31						
Internat. bound'y, Yukon River				25	37	38	56	71	84	87	71	66	52	39	17					
Internat. bound'y, Porcupine River				17	36	33	51	68	79	85			34	34	17					
Head waters Birch Creek				25	26	34	42	68	84	82	70	52	38	28	19					

EXTREMES OF TEMPERATURE—MINIMUM.

Station.	Latitude.	Longitude.	Elevation.	January.	February.	March.	April.	May.	June.	July.	August.	September.	October.	November.	December.	Annual.	Length of record. From	To	Yrs.	Mos.
Coast.																				
Sitka				-1	-3	4	22	27	38	41	41	32	26	5	9					
Pyramid Harbor				-30	-13	-18	14	29	34	39	39	30	21	9	-9					
Ugashik				-27	-21	-39	11	20	28	34	32	22	0	-27	-26					
Unalaska				16	7	5	15	24	34	37	36	33	24	19	12					
St. Michael				-47	-55	-39	-27	-2	22	33	31	18	3	-24	-43					
Point Barrow				-40	-40	-39	-29	-5	20	27	30	5	-21	-31	-38					
Interior.																				
Anvik																				
Nuklukayet				-76	-60	-38	-14	11			28	12	-21	-53	-68					
Fort Reliance				-80	-72	-36	-10	16				18	-11	-50	-69					
Internat. bound'y, Yukon River				-60	-55	-45	-26	8	30	35	31	14	4	-35	-49					
								15	26	36										
Internat. bound'y, Porcupine River				-49	-47	-48	-28						-6	-36	-43					
Kolmakof[1]					-40	-36	9			35	29	5	-14	-31						
Head waters Birch Creek				-31	-31	-21	-2	7	33	40	26	2	-12	-21	-26					

[1] Compiled from Coast Pilot, 1879.

PRECIPITATION (RAIN AND SNOW).

[In inches.]

Station.	Jan.	Feb.	March.	April.	May.	June.	July.	Aug.	Sept.	Oct.	Nov.	Dec.	Annual.	Length of record.
														Years.
Fort Wrangell, 1882	......	9.14	3.90	1.39	1.48	3.40	4.76	2.61	8.06	5.19	18.37	11.49	......	1
Sitka	9.75	10.51	10.02	6.24	4.94	3.58	5.28	6.93	11.00	13.49	13.68	10.11	105.02	7
Juneau	10.17	4.98	7.20	4.49	10.28	5.45	6.41	7.14	7.82	6.25	7.95	7.28	85.43	3
Unalaska	13.81	7.68	6.48	7.51	4.49	4.21	2.78	3.40	8.61	11.98	9.30	11.81	92.14	7
St. Michael	0.86	0.18	0.46	0.49	0.99	1.40	1.75	2.61	2.90	1.34	0.79	0.67	14.44	11
Anvik	1.12	0.40	1.82	0.42	0.52	......	......	......	2.47	1.13	1.41	0.43	......	1
Attu Island	5.19	2.91	2.43	2.16	......	......	......	......	4.06	8.91	6.46	6.52	......	1
Bering Island	0.70	1.59	0.91	1.13	0.95	1.66	2.46	4.62	2.50	2.60	2.96	1.62	21.18	4
Kolmakof	1.26	0.37	1.10	0.88	2.24	......	2.30	2.09	3.83	1.51	2.16	0.57	......	2
Ooglaamie	0.30	0.44	0.32	0.48	0.33	0.47	1.25	4.83	1.10	1.09	0.54	0.32	8.26	2
Fort Reliance	7.40	1.26	1.13	0.08	0.60	......	......	1.46	5.30	0.79	2.93	1.78	......	2
St. Paul Island	3.99	2.51	2.49	2.00	2.39	2.19	4.01	3.61	4.00	5.08	4.16	3.92	40.38	10
Tanana	1.72	1.22	0.40	0.40	0.67	......	......	2.16	1.72	0.50	0.82	0.46	......	1
Ugashik	1.80	0.50	1.04	1.14	1.50	1.14	2.90	4.14	5.32	2.70	1.22	1.38	24.98	3
St. Paul, Kadiak Island	8.01	8.31	10.60	5.52	5.42	5.62	1.49	3.71	5.94	7.14	6.61	9.90	73.27	1

PERIODS DURING WHICH CERTAIN ALASKAN WATERS ARE FREE FROM ICE.

River.	Time of ice breaking.	Time of final freezing.
Yukon:		
Lakes on Lewes..	About June 1, 1898...	About Oct. 5, 1898.
Miles Canyon ...	About April 26, 1898..	
Mouth of Tanana.		Oct. 12, 1898, Oct. 1, 1897 (exceptionally early).
Russian Mission..	May 23 (average of twelve years; extremes, May 15 and June 5).	Nov. 4 (average of five years; extremes, Oct. 30 and Nov. 10).
Port of St. Michael......	May 22, earliest; generally last week in June.	About Oct. 15.
Stikine................	April 28, 1898	
Copper	May 10 (average).....	About Oct. 30.
Sushitna	May 20, 1898	
Matanuska	Middle of May........	Generally in October.

REPORT OF POSTAL SERVICE IN OPERATION IN ALASKA, MARCH 1, 1899.

Postal routes.

STEAMBOAT SERVICE.

No. of route.	From—	To—	Approximate length in miles.	Number of round trips.	Offices supplied.
78,084	San Francisco, Cal..	Dawson, Canada ..	4,408	3 during summer.	Unalaska, St. Michael, Circle, and all Yukon River points.
78,085	Seattle, Wash.......	Dyea, Alaska......	1,000	2 a month...	Skagway.
78,086	Juneau, Alaska	Kadiak, Alaska....	1,150	2 a month, April to Oct.	Sitka, Yakutat, Orca, Seldovia, Tyonek.
78,087	Seldovia, Alaska	Tyonek, Alaska....	110	2 a month, May to Oct.	Sunrise (when steamer lands).
78,088	Sitka, Alaska........	Unalaska, Alaska..	1,030	1 a month for five months, Nov. to March.	Yakutat, Nuchek (n. o.), Orca, Valdez, Seldovia, Kadiak, Karluk, Sandpoint, Unga, Belkofski (n. o.).
78,089	Juneau, Alaska......	Skagway, Alaska..	100	3 a week	Haines, Dyea, Port Townsend, Mary Island, Saxman, Ketchikan, Fort Wrangell, Juneau, Skagway.
78,093	Seattle, Wash.......	Skagway, Alaska..	1,012	2 a month or oftener; usually 5 to 7.	

POSTAL SERVICE IN OPERATION. 137

Postal routes—Continued.

STEAMBOAT SERVICE—Continued.

No. of route.	From—	To—	Approximate length in miles.	Number of round trips.	Offices supplied.
78,094	Seattle, Wash	Dyea, Alaska	1,043	2 a month	Mary Island, Metlakahtla, Fort Wrangell, Juneau, Skagway.
78,095	Seattle, Wash	Dyea, Alaska	1,022	2 a month	Mary Island, Saxman, Ketchikan, Fort Wrangell, Juneau, Skagway.
78,097	Seattle, Wash	Dawson, Canada	4,018	3 trips during summer.	Unalaska, St. Michael, Circle, and all Yukon River points.
78,099	Valdez, Alaska	Nuchek, Alaska	120	2 a month, April 1 to Oct. 31.	Orca.
78,100	Sitka, Alaska	Unalaska, Alaska	1,526	1 a month, April 1 to Oct. 31 each year.	Yakutat, Seldovia, Kadiak, Karluk, Sandpoint, Unga.

STAR SERVICE.

78,101	Fort Wrangell, Alaska.	Jackson, Alaska	195	20 a year	Shakan, Klawock.
78,104	Ketchikan, Alaska	Loring, Alaska	22	2 a month	
78,105	Juneau, Alaska	Tanana, Alaska	1,276	2 a month	Dyea, Sheep Camp, Dawson, Fortymile, Eagle, Star, Circle, Rampart.
78,106	St. Michael, Alaska	Tanana, Alaska	900(?)	1 a month	Kutlik (n. o.), Koserefsky (n. o.), Anvik, Nulato (n. o.), Koyukuk, Nowikakat (n. o.)
78,107	Metlakahtla, Alaska	Ketchikan, Alaska	15	1 a week	
78,108	Chilkat, Alaska	Haines, Alaska	2	1 a week	

Post-offices established.

Anvik.	Juneau.	Metlakahtla.	Sitka.
Chilkat.	Karluk.	Nowikakat.[1]	Skagway.
Circle.	Kenai.[1]	Orca.	Star.
Douglas.	Ketchikan.	Peavy.[1]	Sumdum.
Dyea.	Killisnoo.	Rampart.	Tanana.
Eagle.	Klawock.	St. Michael.	Tyonek.
Fort Wrangell.	Kodiak.	Sandpoint.	Unalaska.
Haines.	Koyukuk.	Saxman.	Unga.
Homer.	Kutlik.[1]	Seldovia.	Yakutat.
Hope.[1]	Loring.	Shakan.	Yukon.[1]
Jackson.	Mary Island.	Sheep Camp.	

[1] Postmasters not commissioned.

UNITED STATES LAND OFFICES.

United States local land offices have been established in Alaska at Circle City, Peavy, Sitka, and Weare, but as yet (Mar. 13, 1899) the only office open for business is at Sitka.

GOLD PRODUCTION OF ALASKA, BY DISTRICTS.[1]

Districts.	1896.	1897.	1898.
Admiralty, Douglas, and Unga islands.	$1,370,861.65	$1,238,082 [a]	Figures not received, but total gold production estimated as about—
Juneau		86,300	
Silver Bow Basin	241,273.73	225,000	
Berners Bay	160,000.00	185,000	
Sumdum	90,171.23	31,890	
Lituya Bay	39,000.00	17,000	
Cook Inlet	120,000.00	191,300	
Norton Sound	15,000.00	15,000	
Yukon River	800,000.00	400,000	
Territorial	25,000.00	50,000	
Totals	$2,861,306.61	$2,439,572	$2,839,572

[1] Taken from reports of the Director of the Mint.   [a] Douglas and Unga.

Wells, Fargo & Co. estimate the total gold production of Alaska for 1898 as $3,321,491.

RATION LIST ADOPTED BY J. E. SPURR.

(For one man one month.)

	Pounds.
Farinaceous food (three-quarters flour)	38¼
Meats and fatty foods (chiefly bacon)	28
Nitrogeneous food (three-quarters beans)	6⅞
Sugar	6
Tea	¾
Dried fruits and vegetables (three-quarters dried fruits)	5
Baking powder (1 lb. to each 35 lbs. of flour) about	1
Salt	¼
Total about	86

1

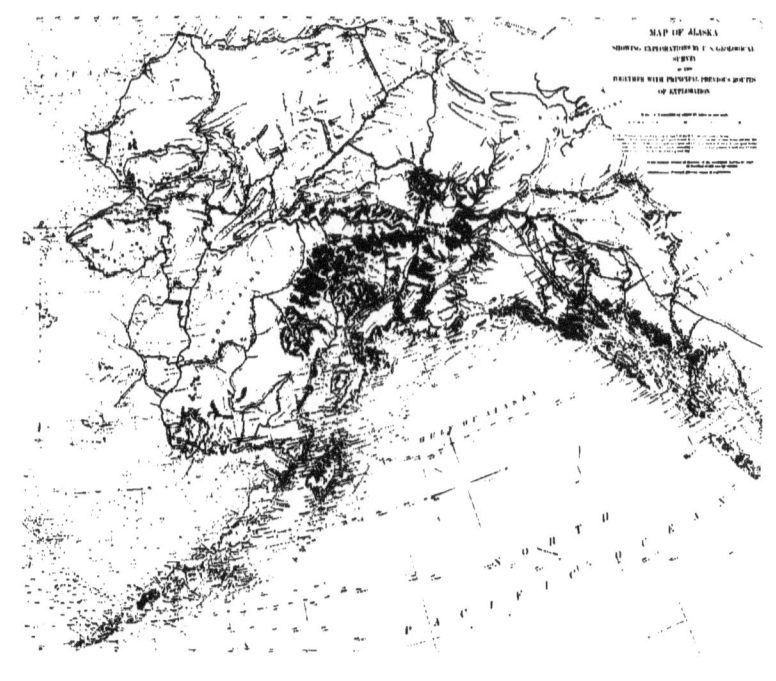

2

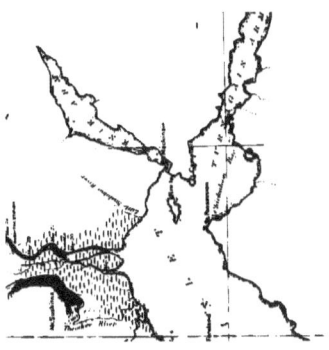

EXPLORATIONS IN
ALASKA
1898
HEADWATERS OF SUSITNA AND
KUSKOKWIM RIVERS,
AND
VICINITY OF KATMAI

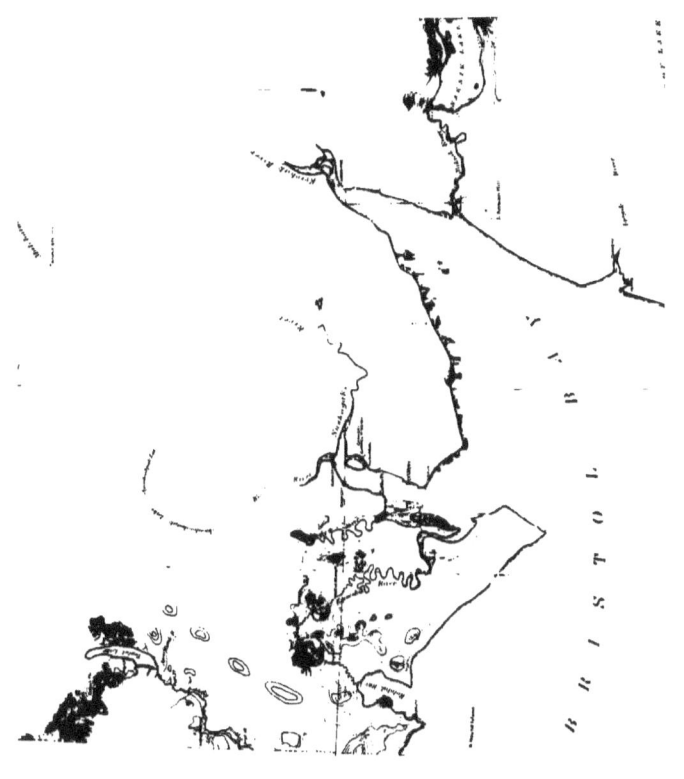

EXPLORATIONS IN
ALANKA
LOWER KUSKOKWIM RIVER, KANEKTOK RIVER,
and
TOGIAK BAY

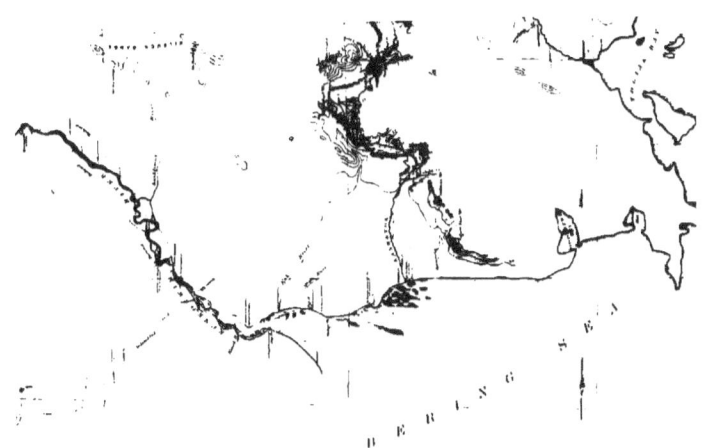

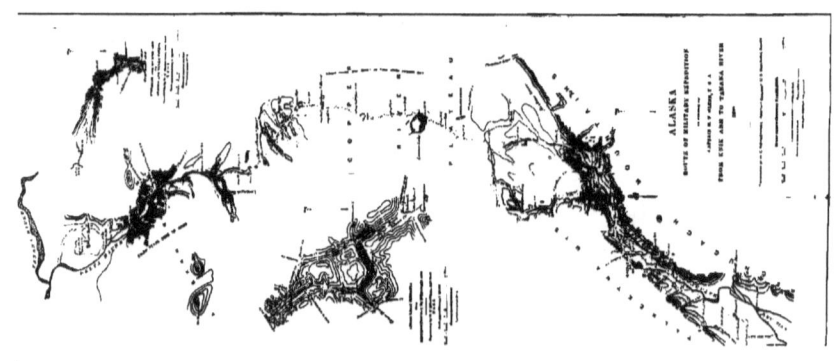

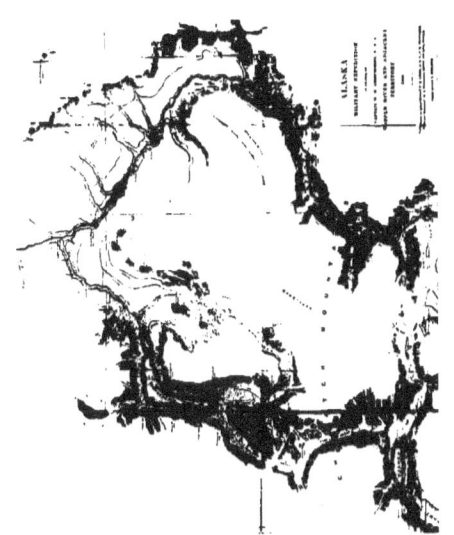

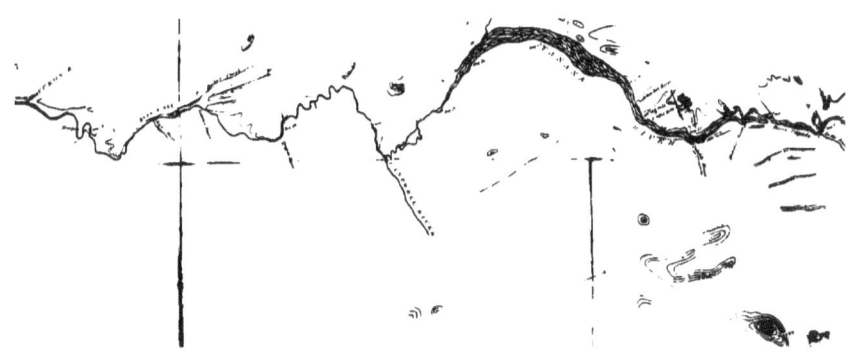

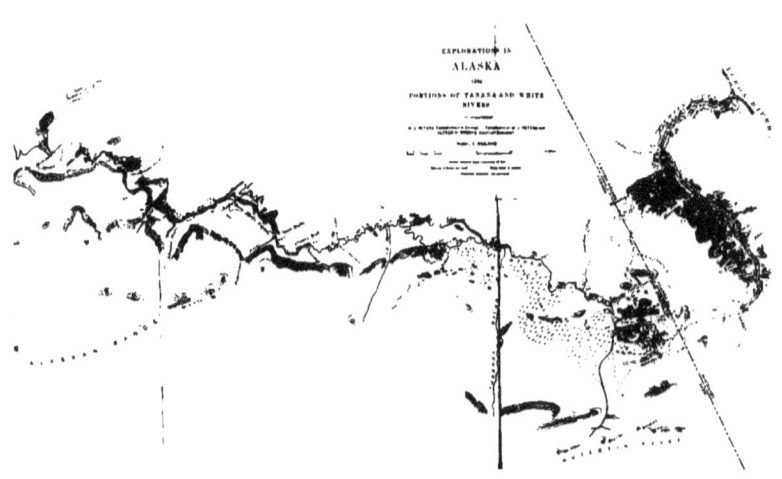

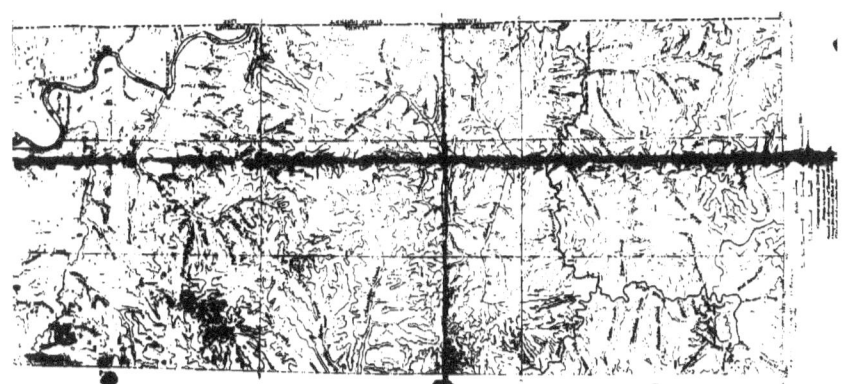

www.ingramcontent.com/pod-product-compliance
Lightning Source LLC
Chambersburg PA
CBHW030332170426
43202CB00010B/1102